ANTI-INFLAMMATORY

Diet Cookbook for Beginners

Strengthen Your Immune System and
Detoxify Your Body by Reducing Inflammation,
with 2000 Days of Quick and Easy Recipes
| Lose Weight and Live Healthy

ADELINE KELLY

In this document, you will find recipes that you can repeat for 2000 days

Table of Contents

INTRODUCTION

In recent times, there has been a lot of discussion regarding the benefits of an anti-inflammatory diet as an alternative method of eating to assist in the fight against inflammation within the body.

Inflammation is a natural response of our immune system, but we tend to think of it as something that should be avoided at all costs. It is important to remember that inflammation is a natural response of our immune system. It shields us from infection and prevents further damage to tissues after an injury, but only under certain conditions.

In this book, we will explain in detail what inflammatory processes are and how they are connected to the diets that are currently considered anti-inflammatory.

CHAPTER ONE
Fundamentals of Anti-Inflammatory Diet

What is inflammation?

Whether it's a bacteria or a virus, an injury from a cut or burn, or exposure to toxins, inflammation is typically a short-term reaction to something our body interprets as harmful. Inflammation can also occur as a result of exposure to toxins.

When our bodies come into contact with an "irritant," a complex chain of chemical reactions begins to take place within them. These reactions cause the classic signs of inflammation, which include swelling, redness, pain, and possibly a loss of tissue function at the injury site.

However, the inflammatory process can become problematic if our immune system cannot effectively suppress it. When this happens, a short-lived but severe reaction risks developing into a persistent illness that lasts longer and harms our health and well-being.

Anti-Inflammatory Diet - Basics?

By reducing the effects of the inflammatory process, an anti-inflammatory diet can help manage symptoms.

The diet restricts some foods while encouraging others and suggests eating at specific times, influencing inflammation in the body.

The anti-inflammatory diet emphasizes eating plant foods and fish, high in healthy fats and phytonutrients while controlling blood sugar levels. The diet aims to influence the control mechanisms that govern the inflammatory process in this way.

Do you know what an anti-inflammatory diet is? Inflammation is the body's natural defense mechanism against infection or tissue damage. When it occurs in any visible part of the body, such as the skin or the throat, we know the symptoms: redness and heating of the affected area.

However, an "invisible" inflammation occurs within the organism and is caused, among other things, by a constant intake of toxins and pro-inflammatory substances and certain lifestyle habits.

As a result, we can say they are foods high in additives or proteins that we cannot digest. In other words, substances that the body does not recognize as food. In response, it alerts leukocytes (white blood cells) to defend against these toxins.

As a result, the body produces more substances that aid in the fight against the infection, resulting in an inflammatory response. However, all of this strains the body, leading to fatigue, headaches, and muscle aches. Furthermore, if left untreated, inflammation can become chronic.

In the long run, a diet high in inflammatory foods can predispose the body to various diseases, including diabetes, cholesterol and triglyceride changes, obesity, and arthritis.

CHAPTER TWO
The Benefits of Anti-Inflammatory Diet

The benefits of following a diet pattern that reduces inflammation are directly connected to improvements in one's health and well-being and longevity. Explore the following scientific studies to learn more about the benefits of maintaining a diet that is high in foods that reduce inflammation and low in foods that cause inflammation:

Diabetes

Diabetes is just one of many chronic conditions that can largely be caused by inflammation. The anti-inflammatory diet, which, as was seen, excludes foods that can stimulate inflammation and includes foods that reduce inflammation, may improve inflammatory biomarkers in diabetics and pre-diabetics. This is because the anti-inflammatory diet excludes foods that can stimulate inflammation and includes foods that reduce inflammation.

Certain types of cancer

Food and inflammatory markers are known to contribute to cancer development. A long-term anti-inflammatory diet may be one way to improve these patient's chances of surviving breast cancer, according to the findings of a study that analyzed the medical histories of 1,064 women who had beat the disease.

Arthritis

THE arthritis Rheumatoid arthritis is a disease that affects the joints, leading to increased inflammation, destruction, loss of function, and disability. One study that investigated whether an anti-inflammatory diet would reduce disease activity observed positive effects on adherence.

Heart Disease

According to the findings of several epidemiological studies, increasing one's consumption of fish, which is high in polyunsaturated fatty acids, is associated with a reduced risk of coronary artery disease and stroke. These effects are a direct consequence of the anti-inflammatory action, which is the primary factor in lowering the risk of developing atherosclerosis.

Anti-inflammatory diet foods

The good news is that just like foods that cause inflammation, some interfere with the process and reduce its severity. They behave in this manner because they can boost the release of hormones that inhibit or even block the action of inflammatory agents. In other words, they can suppress the inflammatory response.

Learn about the foods that can help reduce inflammation in your diet:

- Fish with omega-3: salmon, tuna, herring, sardines, and mackerel.
- Oilseeds: chestnuts, nuts, and almonds.
- Whole grains and seeds: chia, linseed, sesame, wheat germ, quinoa, amaranth. Fruits rich in vitamin C: orange, kiwi, acerola, lemon, guava, tangerine, passion fruit, cashew, melon, tangerine, papaya, and acerola.
- Red fruits: strawberry, pomegranate, watermelon, cherry, and grape.
- Oils: extra virgin olive oil and coconut oil.
- Vegetables and vegetables: ginger, cauliflower, turnip, radish, cabbage, carrot, pumpkin, spinach, arugula, broccoli, watercress, escarole, and kale.

- Teas: green tea, rosemary tea, ginger tea, fennel tea.

- Foods that have monounsaturated fats (omega-9): olives, and avocados.

- Ginger: rich in vitamins C, B6 and with bactericidal action, it helps to strengthen the immune system.

- Yam: because it increases the body's defenses, has anti-inflammatory action, is rich in vitamin C, complex B, minerals, and beta-carotene, has antioxidant action helping to eliminate toxins from the body.

- Garlic and onion: both have large amounts of antioxidants and anti-inflammatories;

- Spices: saffron, and curry.

- Bitter chocolate.

- Pepper and chili.

- Red wine, in moderation.

- Finally, probiotics: kefir, some types of yogurt, and kombucha.

Foods Forbidden on the Anti-Inflammatory Diet

On the other hand, knowledge of the foods that contribute to inflammation is also interesting. As a result, they should not be included in a diet designed to reduce inflammation, or their consumption should be restricted:

- Ultra-processed products: as they contain chemical substances, dyes, preservatives, flavorings, and flavors that cause inflammation.

- Foods rich in omega-6: oils extracted from soybeans, cotton, corn, canola, and sunflowers are examples of vegetable oils. If you cannot eliminate these foods from your diet, you should try to find a healthy middle ground by increasing your intake of omega-3 fatty acids. The following are possible ways to proceed: one serving of omega 3 for every two, with a maximum of four out of six servings. That is, increase your consumption of fish like sardines, tuna, and salmon, as well as seeds and grains like chia and linseed, and reduce your consumption of oils that have omega 6, as well as industrialized products in which they appear as an ingredient; in other words, increase your consumption of omega-3-rich foods.

- Refined cereals: bread, pasta, white rice, biscuits, wheat, cornstarch, cornmeal. However, these foods do not need to be cut out of the diet, but replaced with whole versions.

- Soda and sugary juices, alcoholic beverages (but except wine in moderation).

- Meat: pork and beef with a lot of fat.

- Sausages: sausage, sausage, bacon, salami, mortadella, and preserves with salt.

- Whole milk, yellow cheese, cream, and excess butter.

- Industrialized sweets, biscuits, cakes and ice cream.

- Trans fats: i.e. foods with "partially hydrogenated" in the ingredients list.

BREAKFAST RECIPES

1. Sweet Potato Hash

Preparation time: 15 minutes
Cooking time: 15 minutes
Servings: 4

Ingredient:

- 2 spoons of coconut oil
- ½ onion, cut into thin slices
- 1 cup sliced mushrooms
- 1 clove of garlic, thinly sliced
- 2 large sweet potatoes, cooked and cut into ½-inch cubes
- 1 cup finely chopped chard
- ½ cup of vegetable broth
- ¼ tsp freshly ground pepper
- 1 tbsp minced fresh thyme
- 1 tbsp minced fresh parsley

Preparation:

1. The coconut oil should be melted in a large skillet over high heat.
2. To the pan, add the mushrooms, onion, and garlic. Sauté the onions and mushrooms for about 8 minutes or until they reach the desired level of tenderness.
3. Add the Swiss chard, sweet potatoes, and vegetable broth to the skillet. Wait 5 minutes before serving.
4. Pepper, thyme, and sage should all be stirred at this point.

Nutritional value Calories: 212, Fat: 7g, Carbohydrates: 35g, Protein: 30g.

2. Mushroom Frittata

Preparation time: 15 minutes
Cooking time: 20 minutes
Servings: 4

Ingredient:

- 1½ cups chickpea flour
- 1½ cups of water
- 2 tbsp of extra virgin olive oil
- 1 small red onion, diced
- 20 oz of sliced mushrooms
- 1 tsp ground turmeric
- ½ tsp ground cumin
- ½ tsp freshly ground black pepper
- 2 tbsp chopped fresh parsley

Preparation:

1. Turn the oven up to 350 °F.
2. Mix the water and chickpea flour in a small bowl using a whisk until the mixture is smooth and set aside.
3. Olive oil should be heated to a high temperature in a large skillet made of cast iron or one that can go in the oven. After the oil has been heated, add the onion to the pan. Sauté the onion for three to five minutes or until it has become softer and slightly translucent. After adding the mushrooms, continue to sauté for another five minutes. After adding the turmeric, cumin, and pepper, continue to sauté the mixture for an additional minute.
4. The batter will be poured over the vegetables, and the parsley will be sprinkled. Put the skillet in an oven that has been preheated and bake it for twenty to twenty-five minutes.
5. Prepare and serve either hot or at room temperature.

Nutritional value Calories: 240, Fat: 8g, Carbohydrates: 34g, Protein: 11g.

3. Grapefruit Breakfast

Preparation time: 5 minutes
Servings: 1

Ingredient:

- 2 slices Canadian bacon
- 1 piece grapefruit
- ½ cup 0% fat Greek yogurt
- 1/3 cup blueberries
- 3 ½ tbsp. sliced almonds

Preparation:

1. Take the slices of Canadian bacon and cut them into more manageable chunks. To reheat, place the dish in the microwave oven.
2. First, divide the grapefruit in half lengthwise, then cut each half into thinner slices. Put the pieces in a bowl to hold them. Combine the Canadian bacon with the sauce.
3. The next step is to get another bowl and combine the yogurt, almonds, and blueberries.
4. The contents of the two bowls should be combined and thoroughly mixed together.
5. Serve, and have fun with it!

Nutritional value Calories: 74, Carbohydrates: 19g, Fat 13g, Protein 6g.

4. Eggs and Fruit Salad

Preparation time: 20 minutes
Servings: 1

Ingredient:

- ½ cup sliced strawberries
- ½ cup tangerine sections, unsweetened or fresh
- ½ cup blueberries
- Egg whites (6 boiled eggs, discard yolks)
- ½ cup avocado
- 3 tbsp parsley

Preparation:

1. Make the fruit salad in a bowl about the same size as the serving dish. Strawberry slices are added to a bowl with blueberries, mandarin orange sections, and gentle mixing.
2. Eggs should be boiled for approximately ten minutes, after which they should be allowed to cool. Cut the eggs in half lengthwise and scoop out the yolks.
3. Prepare the egg whites and avocado by dicing them and then combining them in a separate bowl. Mix in the salsa thoroughly.
4. Put some fruit salad sidings, and serve.

Nutritional value Calories: 74, Carbohydrates: 19g, Fat 13g, Protein 6g.

5. Spinach Muffins

Preparation time: 15 minutes
Cooking time: 15 minutes
Servings: 12

Ingredient:

- Cooking spray
- 2 cups packed spinach
- 2 eggs
- ¼ cup of raw honey
- 3 tbsp of extra virgin olive oil
- 1 tsp vanilla extract
- 1 cup oat flour
- 1 cup almond flour
- 2 tsp of baking powder
- 1 tsp of bicarbonate of soda
- Pinch of freshly ground black pepper

Preparation:

1. Turn the oven up to 350 °F.
2. Spraying 12 muffin cups with cooking spray will either line or grease them.
3. Spinach, eggs, honey, olive oil, and vanilla extract should be mixed in a food processor. To a smooth consistency, process.
4. Mix the oat flour, almond flour, baking powder, baking soda, and pepper in a medium bowl using a whisk. Place the spinach mixture in the bowl, then give it a thorough stir.
5. Put two-thirds of the batter into each muffin cup. Put the muffins in an oven preheated to 350 °F and bake them for about 15 minutes until they have a golden brown color and a firm texture.
6. Before attempting to take the muffins out of the tin, move the pan to a cooling rack and give it ten minutes to cool down completely.

Nutritional value Calories: 108, Fat: 6g, Carbohydrates: 12g, Protein: 3g.

6. Coconut Pancakes

Preparation time: 10 minutes
Cooking time: about 5 minutes per pancake
Servings: 4

Ingredient:

- 4 eggs
- 1 cup coconut or almond milk, plus additional as needed
- 1 tbsp melted coconut oil or almond butter, plus more for greasing the pan
- 1 tbsp maple syrup
- 1 tsp vanilla extract
- ½ cup coconut flour
- 1 tsp of bicarbonate of soda

Preparation:

1. With the help of an electric mixer, combine the eggs, coconut milk, coconut oil, maple syrup, and vanilla extract in a bowl of medium size.
2. In a low-volume bowl, combine the dry ingredients of baking soda, and coconut flour by stirring. Mix the dry and wet ingredients while beating vigorously until the mixture is lump-free and smooth.
3. If the batter is too thick, you can thin it out by adding more liquid until it reaches the consistency of the standard pancake batter.
4. Coconut oil should be used to lightly grease a large skillet. Put it over heat that's between medium and high.
5. Cook the pancakes for about three minutes, or until the bottom is golden brown, using scoops of batter measuring half a cup each. Cook the other side for about two minutes after you've flipped it.
6. While you cook the remaining pancake batter, stack the completed pancakes on a plate. This recipe yields approximately eight pancakes.

Nutritional value Calories: 193, Fat: 11g, Carbohydrates: 15g, Protein: 9g.

7. Eggs and Apple Pork with Strawberries

Preparation time: 15 minutes
Servings: 1

Ingredient:

- Olive oil (1 ½ tsp - divided)
- 2 oz boneless center-cut sirloin pork chops
- 1 small apple, sliced
- ¼ tsp cinnamon
- ½ cup egg white
- 1 cup sliced strawberries

Preparation:

1. Bring half a teaspoon's worth of olive oil to medium-high heat in a large skillet. Place the pork, seasoned with pepper, and apple slices, which have been seasoned with cinnamon, on opposite sides of the skillet. Cook the pork and apple slices until the pork is no longer pink and the apple slices are slightly pliable.
2. Take the pork and apple slices out of the skillet and put them to the side for later. Keep warm.
3. Egg whites should be scrambled while the remaining one teaspoon of olive oil is heated.
4. Add some sliced strawberries to the dish as a garnish and serve them on the side.
5. Serve, and have fun with it!

Nutritional value Calories: 120, Fat: 7g, Carbohydrates: 15g, Protein: 15g.

8. Oatmeal Spiced with Apple Pie

Preparation time: 45 minutes
Servings: 4

Ingredient:

- 3 cups water
- ¾ cup steel-cut oats
- 2 tsp pumpkin spice - pumpkin pie spice
- 3 oz zone protein powder
- 1 cup apple sauce
- 1 tsp stevia extract, to taste
- 16 pecans or walnuts 16 pieces – halves

Preparation:

1. Bring the water to a boil, add the pumpkin pie spice and steel-cut oats and stir to combine. Once it has been cooking for about five minutes, turn the heat down. Maintain a low simmer for thirty minutes. Wait until the dish has cooled down completely before mixing in the protein powder. (You can make this the night before, store it in the refrigerator, and then all you have to do to reheat it the next morning is put it in the microwave.) When you are almost ready to eat, add the remaining components to the dish.
2. If the dish was prepared the night before, remove it from the refrigerator, take it out, and divide it into four separate bowls. After dividing the remaining ingredients between the four bowls, please place them in the microwave oven and set them to the highest temperature for 2 minutes and 15 seconds. Mix it up while it's about halfway done.

Nutritional value Calories 356, Total Fat 12g, Carbohydrates 38g, Protein 25g.

9. Chocolate Cherry Smoothie

Preparation time: 5 min
Servings: 2

Ingredient:

- 1 tbsp unprocessed, unsweetened cocoa powder
- ½ cup frozen dark cherries, pitted
- 1 cup coconut, almond, or flaxseed milk
- ½ tsp pure vanilla extract; a few drops of liquid stevia, preferably sweet leaf vanilla crème
- Ice cubes, if desired

Preparation:

1. Use a blender to combine all of the ingredients. Continue to process until there are no lumps left.
2. Pour the contents into a tall glass.
3. Serve, and have fun with it!

Nutritional value Calories: 162 Fat: 2.5 g Carbohydrate: 37.6g, Protein: 3.6g.

10. Orange Apple Breakfast Shake

- **Preparation time:** 10 minutes
- **Servings:** 1

Ingredient:

- 2 tbsp almonds
- ½ cup apple slices
- ½ cup orange sections
- 1 cup 2% milk
- ½ oz zone protein powder

Preparation:

1. Put all of the ingredients in the blender at the same time. Continue to combine everything until it is uniformly combined and smooth.
2. The contents of the blender should be poured into a large glass.
3. Serve, and have fun with it!

Nutritional value Calories: 337, Fat: 11g, Carbohydrates: 35g, Protein: 26g.

11. Gingerbread Oatmeal

Preparation time: 10 minutes
Cooking time: 10 minutes
Servings: 1

Ingredient:

- 1 cup water
- ½ cup old-fashioned oatmeal
- ¼ cup unsweetened dried cranberries or cherries
- 1 tsp ground ginger
- ½ tsp cinnamon powder
- ¼ tsp ground nutmeg
- 1 tbsp flaxseed
- 1 tbsp molasses

Preparation:

1. In a saucepan of appropriate size, combine the water, oats, cranberries or cherries, ginger, cinnamon, and nutmeg. Bring the mixture to a boil over medium-high heat. Bring the mixture to a boil, then turn the heat to a simmer. Continue to simmer for another 5 minutes, until almost all the water has been absorbed, whichever comes first.
2. Place the flaxseeds in the saucepan and then cover it. Allow the mixture to sit for an additional five minutes.
3. Before serving, finish the dish with a few drizzles of molasses.

Nutritional value Calories: 98, Fat: 5g, Carbohydrates: 16g, Protein: 6g.

12. Buckwheat Waffles

Preparation time: 15 minutes
Cooking time: about 6 minutes per waffle
Servings: 4

Ingredient:

- 1½ cups wheat flour
- ½ cup brown rice flour
- 2 tsp of baking powder
- 1 tsp of bicarbonate of soda
- 1 egg
- 1 tsp of maple syrup
- 2 tsp of vanilla extract
- 1 cup of water
- 1½ cups almond milk
- Coconut oil for the waffle iron

Preparation:

1. Mix the buckwheat flour, rice flour, baking powder, and baking soda in a medium bowl using a whisk.
2. Add the egg, maple syrup, and vanilla extract to the dry ingredients and mix well. Stir in the water and almond milk in a slow and steady stream, stirring until the batter is completely smooth.
3. Allow the batter to sit for ten minutes to become slightly thicker.
4. After sitting for some time, the buckwheat might fall to the bottom of the bowl; therefore, you should stir it before using it.
5. The waffle iron should be heated, then brushed with coconut oil before use.
6. Cook the waffles following the instructions provided by the manufacturer after adding the batter to the waffle iron.

Nutritional value Calories: 282, Fat: 4g, Carbohydrates: 55g, Protein: 9g.

13. Buckwheat Crepes with Berries

Preparation time: 15 minutes
Cooking time: 5 minutes per crêpe
Servings: 6

Ingredient:

- 1 cup wheat flour
- 2 tbsp coconut oil (1 tbsp melted)
- 1 ½ cups almond milk or water
- 1 egg
- 1 tsp vanilla extract
- 3 cups fresh fruit, divided
- 6 tbsp chia jam, divided

Preparation:

1. In a small bowl, combine the buckwheat flour, one tablespoon of melted coconut oil, almond milk, egg, and vanilla extract by whisking the ingredients together.
2. The remaining one tablespoon of coconut oil should be melted in a large nonstick skillet measuring 12 inches in diameter over medium-high heat. Turn the pan to ensure that the melted oil covers it in an even layer.
3. Pour a quarter of a cup of the batter into the pan. Turn the skillet so that the batter can cover the entire surface.
4. Cook for two minutes until the sides start turning in on themselves. Turn the crêpe over with a spatula, and cook it on the other side for one minute. Place the crêpe on a plate for serving. Crêpes should be made with the remaining batter throughout the process. You ought to have between four and six crêpes.
5. Put one crepe on a plate and top it with a half cup's worth of berries and one tablespoon's chia jam. After you have added the filling, fold the crepe over it. Continue in this manner with the remaining crepes, and then serve.

Nutritional value Calories: 242, Fat: 11g, Carbohydrates: 33g, Protein: 7g.

14. Spicy Quinoa

Preparation time: 10 minutes
Cooking time: 20 minutes
Servings: 4

Ingredient:

- 1 cup quinoa, rinsed well
- 2 cups of water
- ½ cup grated coconut
- ¼ cup hemp seeds
- 2 spoons of flaxseed
- 1 tsp cinnamon powder
- 1 tsp vanilla extract
- 1 cup fresh fruit of your choice, divided
- ¼ cup chopped hazelnuts

Preparation:

1. Mix the quinoa and water in a medium saucepan and cook them over high heat.
2. Bring to a boil, then immediately lower the heat to a simmer and continue cooking for 15 to 20 minutes, or until the quinoa is completely cooked (it should double or triple in bulk, similar to couscous, and be slightly translucent).
3. Mix in the flaxseed, coconut, hemp seeds, cinnamon, and vanilla extract until well combined.
4. After dividing the quinoa between four bowls, garnish each serving with one-fourth of a cup of berries and one tablespoon of hazelnuts.

Nutritional value Calories: 286, Fat: 13g, Carbohydrates: 32g, Protein: 10g.

SOUPS AND SALADS RECIPES

15. Sweet Potato and Rice Soup

Preparation time: 15 minutes
Cooking time: 15 minutes
Servings: 4

Ingredient:

- 4 cups of vegetable broth
- 1 large sweet potato, peeled and cut into 1-inch cubes
- 2 onions, coarsely chopped
- 2 garlic cloves, thinly sliced
- 2 tsp minced fresh ginger
- 1 bunch of broccoli, cut into 1-inch pieces
- 1 cup cooked basmati rice
- ¼ cup fresh coriander leaves

Preparation:

1. Put the broth in a large Dutch oven that has been preheated to high heat, and bring it to a boil.
2. In a large bowl, combine the sweet potato, onion, garlic, and ginger. Keep the sweet potato at a simmer for five to eight minutes, or until it is completely cooked.
3. After adding the broccolini, continue to simmer the mixture for three more minutes.
4. Take the pan away from the heat immediately. Rice and cilantro should be stirred in together.

Nutritional value Calories: 167, Fat: 2g, Carbohydrates: 29g, Protein: 8g.

16. Broccoli and Lentil Stew

Preparation time: 15 minutes
Cooking time: 30 minutes
Servings: 4

Ingredient:

- 1 tbsp extra virgin olive oil, plus additional for drizzling
- 1 small onion, finely chopped
- 1 small carrot, chopped
- 2 garlic cloves, minced
- 2 cups of vegetable broth
- 1 cup dried green or brown lentils
- 1 tsp dried oregano
- 6 cups broccoli florets
- ¼ tsp freshly ground black pepper
- ½ cup chopped pitted green olives
- ¼ cup chopped fresh Italian parsley

Preparation:

1. The olive oil should be heated in a large saucepan over high heat.
2. To the pan, add the carrot, onion, and garlic. Sauté for 5 minutes.
3. After adding the lentils, vegetable broth, and oregano, bring the mixture to a boil. Bring the temperature down to a simmer. Maintain a simmer in the soup for 15 to 20 minutes, or until the lentils reach the desired degree of doneness.
4. After adding the broccoli, cover the pot and continue to simmer the mixture for another 5 minutes.
5. Take the pot off the heat and stir in the olives and parsley before returning it to the oven. Add a little water and stir it if the soup is too thick.
6. Place a serving of the soup in each bowl, top with a sprinkling of olive oil, and then serve.

Nutritional value Calories: 182, Fat: 6g, Carbohydrates: 24g, Protein: 11g..

17. Quick and Easy Pumpkin Soup

Preparation time: 5 minutes
Cooking time: 10 minutes
Servings: 4

Ingredient:

- 1 cup chopped onion
- 1-inch. eeled and chopped ginger root
- 1 clove minced garlic
- 6 cups vegetable stock
- 4 cups pumpkin puree
- ½ tsp chopped thyme
- ½ cup milk half and half
- 1 tsp chopped parsley

Preparation:

1. Place the garlic, ginger, and onion in a heavy-bottomed soup pot. After adding a half cup of vegetable stock, continue cooking for 5 minutes, or until the onion is fork tender.
2. Combine pumpkin puree, thyme and 5 12 cups vegetable stock in a pot. Stir to combine. Prepare the soup by simmering it for half an hour.
3. Using a hand blender, bring the soup to a smooth consistency so it can be served.
4. Take the soup off the heat and stir the half-and-half milk in a separate bowl. After thoroughly stirring, sprinkle some chopped parsley on top as a garnish and serve.

Nutritional value Calories: 242, Fat: 11g, Carbohydrates: 33g, Protein: 7g.

18. Baked Sweet Potato Soup

Preparation time: 10 minutes
Cooking time: 30 minutes
Servings: 4

Ingredient:

- 2 ½ lbs sweet potatoes
- 1 tbsp extra virgin olive oil
- ½ tsp freshly ground pepper
- 1 ½ cups chopped leeks or onions
- 1 tsp chopped garlic
- ½ cup white wine
- 1 tsp chopped thyme leaves
- 5 cups vegetable broth
- 2 cups orange juice

Preparation:

1. Turn the oven on to 400 °F before you put anything in it. Sweet potatoes should be peeled and then cut into very small pieces.
2. After spreading the sweet potatoes out on a baking sheet, season them with pepper, and olive oil before baking them. Cook the potatoes in the oven at 400 °F for forty-five to fifty minutes, or until the sweet potatoes are nicely browned. Set aside.
3. Cook the leeks or onions in a large soup pot over medium to high heat for about eight minutes, or until they reach the desired tenderness. After adding the ginger and garlic, stir and cook for an additional minute. After adding the white wine, boil the mixture and cook until it has completely evaporated.
4. After the wine has been completely consumed, add the sweet potatoes, thyme, and vegetable broth before bringing the entire soup mixture to a boil. Reduce the heat and let it simmer for approximately twenty minutes, or until the vegetables have reached the desired softness and tenderness. Make sure to work in batches using a blender to puree the soup. Before serving, bring each pot of soup back up to temperature.

Nutritional value Calories: 108, Fat: 6g, Carbohydrates: 12g, Protein: 3g.

19. Cauliflower Soup with Roasted Garlic

Preparation time: 10 minutes
Cooking time: 1 hour
Servings: 4

Ingredient:

- 1 large head cauliflower about 2 ½ lb.
- 4 ½ tsp olive oil
- 3 unpeeled garlic cloves
- 3 cups reduced-sodium chicken broth
- 1 cup 2% reduced-fat milk
- ½ cup grated manchego or parmesan cheese
- Freshly ground black pepper
- Garnishes: olive oil, pomegranate seeds, fresh thyme leaves

Preparation:

1. Prepare the oven to 425 °F. Cut the cauliflower into florets that are about 2 inches long and toss them with olive oil. Prepare a jelly-roll pan by spreading the florets out in a single layer. Garlic cloves should be individually wrapped in aluminum foil before being placed on the jelly-roll pan with the cauliflower.
2. Bake the cauliflower in an oven preheated to 425 °F for 30 to 40 minutes, or until it reaches a golden brown color, turning it over once every 15 minutes.
3. Cauliflower should now be placed in a large Dutch oven. Unwrap the garlic and allow it to rest for five minutes. Garlic should be peeled before being added to the cauliflower. After adding the stock and bringing it to a simmer over medium heat, cook for another 5 minutes while stirring the pot occasionally. Let mixture cool for 10 minutes.
4. Blend the cauliflower mixture, working in batches if necessary, until it is completely smooth, stopping to scrape down the sides of the blender as necessary.
5. Bring the cauliflower mixture back into the Dutch oven, and then stir in the milk and cheese, Cook for two to three minutes over low heat, stirring occasionally, or until the food is completely warmed. Pepper should be added to taste.

Nutritional value Calories: 306, Carbohydrates: 17g, Protein: 11g, Fat: 23g.

20. Vegetable Soup

Preparation time: 15 minutes
Cooking time: 40 minutes
Servings: 4

Ingredient:

- 2 cups chopped fresh tomatoes or crushed canned tomatoes
- 1 can chickpeas (14 to 16 oz), rinsed and drained
- 4 medium carrots, peeled and chopped about 1 cup
- 2 medium potatoes, peeled and chopped about 1-1/2 cups
- 2 medium chopped onions about 1 cup
- 2 large celery stalks, chopped about 1 cup
- 2 garlic cloves, minced
- 1 large red bell pepper, chopped about 1 cup
- 1 medium zucchini, chopped about 1-1/2 cups
- 6 cups of water
- Freshly ground black pepper
- ½ cup long-grain white rice
- 1 cup chopped fresh basil
- Extra virgin olive oil, to serve, if desired
- Freshly grated Parmesan cheese, to serve, if desired

Preparation:

1. The Perfect Simmer Cooker Size: 5 to 6-Quart
2. Tomatoes, garbanzo beans, carrots, potatoes, onions, celery, garlic, bell pepper, zucchini, water, and ground black pepper to taste should be mixed in a bowl and stirred thoroughly.
3. Cook, covered, on LOW for 8–9 hours or on HIGH for 4–5 hours, or until the vegetables are tender, whichever comes first, until the vegetables are tender.
4. Mix in the rice thoroughly. Cover and continue cooking on HIGH for 30 minutes, until the rice is cooked through and the soup thickens.
5. After stirring in the basil, allow the soup to come to room temperature before serving.

6. Place the soup in the bowls. Taste, then season to taste with additional pepper as desired. You can serve it with a drizzle of olive oil and some Parmesan on top before serving.

Nutritional value Calories: 198, Fat: 5g, Protein: 7g, Carbohydrates: 31g.

21. Deli Soup and a Roll

Preparation time: 20 min
Cooking time: 30 minutes
Serving: 4

Ingredient:

- Tomato soup sauce
- 2 tbsp olive oil
- ¼ cup chopped onion (about half a small onion)
- 1 clove of minced garlic
- 1 tsp of honey
- ¼ tsp black pepper
- ¼ tsp dried basil
- ¼ tsp dried oregano
- ¼ tsp thyme
- 14 oz diced canned tomatoes with juices
- 1 cup vegetable or chicken broth
- 1 tsp balsamic vinegar
- 8 cabbage leaves
- 10 oz ground beef
- 4 oz parmesan cheese
- 3 eggs
- 4 slices of whole wheat bread
- 3 tbsp breadcrumbs
- 1 cup milk

Preparation:

For the sauce

1. Warm the oil up in a Dutch oven of sufficient size until it is hot. After adding the onion, cook it for 5–8 minutes, or until it is soft. After adding the garlic, continue to cook for one minute. The honey, pepper, basil, oregano, and thyme should all be added at this point. Mix everything, then continue cooking for another 5 minutes.

To the tomatoes, add the broth, and finish with the vinegar. Bring to a boil, reduce heat to low and continue cooking for another half an hour.

2. Place the soup mixture inside a blender and process it until it is completely smooth. Be very careful, because the mixture is already hot, and the blender will cause it to expand significantly when it is turned on. Puree in two separate batches if necessary.

For the roll-ups

1. Wash the savoy cabbage leaves and blanch them for a few minutes. Drain and pat dry.

2. Put the mince, eggs, bread soaked in milk and Parmesan cheese in a bowl and mix well, whisking everything together. If you find it too soft you can add a little bread crumbs. Stuff the cabbage leaves by placing a spoonful of mixture in the center of each leaf, wrap it up by closing the flaps. Place the rolls back on a baking sheet sprinkled with Parmesan cheese and breadcrumbs.

3. Drizzle olive oil over the top and bake for 30 minutes at 360 °F. After cooking the food should be transferred to a plate, serve hot accompanied by the dipping sauce.

Nutritional value Calories: 410, Fat: 45g, Protein: 34g, Carbohydrates: 22g.

22. Antipasto Salad

Preparation time: 15 minutes
Total time: 15 minutes
Serving: 8

Ingredient:

- 1 ½ head of shredded iceberg lettuce
- 2 cups of celery sliced
- ¾ cup of carrots thinly sliced
- 3 cups sliced mushrooms
- 1 cup onions, in half rings
- 2 ¼ cups of red bell pepper, in half rings
- ¾ cup of chickpeas, canned
- 2 oz light tuna chunks, in water
- 2 oz low-fat mozzarella cheese, grated
- 3 oz sliced turkey
- 2 oz extra-lean ham slice
- 2 tsp dried basil - crushed in the palm
- 3 tsp extra virgin olive oil, drizzle
- ¼ cup of fat-free savory sauce

Preparation:

1. Obtain three plates with an oval shapes that are large and place a bed of lettuce on each one. Place the carrots, celery, mushrooms, red pepper, onions, and garbanzo beans on top of the bed of lettuce so that they form a vertical line beginning on the right side of the plate and ending on the left side.
2. After that, place the cheese, tuna, ham, and turkey on the plates in an even distribution, and then use the strips of red bell pepper as dividers between the different types of meat.
3. Crush the basil between the palms of your hands to release its vibrant freshness, and then sprinkle it over the plates. On each of the plates, sprinkle one teaspoon of olive oil. Before pouring the dressing over the salad, could you give it a quick whisking

Nutritional value Calories: 356, Fat: 12g, Carbohydrates: 38g, Protein: 25g.

23. Eggs and Fruit Salad

Preparation time: 20 minutes
Servings: 1

Ingredient

- ½ cup sliced strawberries
- ½ cup tangerine sections, unsweetened or fresh
- ½ cup blueberries
- Egg whites (6 boiled eggs, discard yolks)
- ½ cup avocado
- 3 tsp parsley

Preparation

1. Make the fruit salad in a bowl about the same size as the serving dish. Strawberry slices are added to a bowl with blueberries, mandarin orange sections, and gentle mixing.
2. Eggs should be boiled for approximately ten minutes, after which they should be allowed to cool. Cut the eggs in half lengthwise and scoop out the yolks.
3. Prepare the egg whites and avocado by dicing them and then combining them in a separate bowl. Mix in the salsa thoroughly.
4. Put some fruit salad sidings, and serve.

Nutritional value Calories: 74, Carbohydrates: 19g, Fat: 13g, Protein: 6g.

24. Persimmon and Pear Salad

Preparation time: 15 minutes
Servings: 6

Ingredient:

- 1 tsp whole-grain mustard
- 2 tbsp lemon juice
- 3 tbsp extra virgin olive oil
- 1 pc chopped shallot
- 1 tsp minced garlic
- 1 pc. sliced ripe persimmon.
- 1 pc. sliced ripe pear
- ½ cup roasted and chopped pecans
- 6 cup baby spinach

Preparation:

1. In a salad bowl, combine the shallot, garlic, mustard, lemon juice, and olive oil by whisking them together.
2. Incorporate pears, persimmons, spinach, and pecans into the salad ingredients. Toss the fruits and vegetables thoroughly so that they are covered.
3. Immediately serve after cooking. Keep the leftovers in a container that doesn't let air in.

Nutritional value Calories 350, Carbohydrates 25g, Fat 1.5g, Protein 3g.

25. Arlecchino salad

Preparation time: 15 min
Servings: 2

Ingredient:

- 1 ½ tsp extra virgin olive oil
- 3 tbsp freshly squeezed lemon juice
- 1 tsp lemon pepper
- 2 cups romaine lettuce, torn
- 1 cup sliced strawberries
- 1 ½ cups sliced cucumber
- 1 cup cherry tomatoes, halved
- ½ cup sliced mushrooms
- 1 tsp cashews, crushed
- 3 oz piece of light tuna in water
- 2 pcs. Melba toast, crushed like croutons

Preparation:

1. In a bowl of appropriate size, make the dressing by combining the extra virgin olive oil, lemon pepper, and lemon juice by whisking them together.
2. Use the ingredients (including the toasts) to make a salad with the remaining components. Combine all ingredients in a bowl, then sprinkle the top with the melba toast crumbs.
3. Just before serving, pour on the dressing.

Nutritional value Calories: 41, Carbohydrates: 6.1g, Fat: 0.5g, Protein: 1.8g.

26. Barbecue Chicken Salad

Preparation time: 30 minutes
Servings: 4

Ingredient:

- 2 tsp olive oil
- 3 oz boneless chicken breast, diced
- 1 ½ cups bell peppers, strips
- ¼ cup diced onions
- 1/8   tsp cider vinegar
- 1/8 tsp Worcestershire sauce
- 1 tsp minced garlic
- ½ cup zoned barbecue sauce
- 3 cups lettuce
- 2 cups shredded cabbage

Preparation:

1. Place the chicken breasts, oil, pepper, vinegar, onion, garlic, and Worcestershire sauce in a saute pan. Saute over medium heat until the chicken is cooked through. After browning the chicken and making sure the vegetables are cooked through, add some Zoned barbecue sauce and continue cooking.
2. Keep the lid on the pan and let it simmer for about five minutes, or until it reaches the desired temperature, stirring it every so often to ensure the flavors can combine successfully.
3. Combine the shredded cabbage and the lettuce in a bowl, and then place the salad-cabbage mixture on an oval plate that is quite large. Place the chicken and the vegetable mixture in the middle of the plate. Place the salad cabbage mixture underneath the chicken and vegetable mixture.
4. After giving the dish a light dusting of pepper, serve it as soon as possible.

Nutritional value Calories: 308kcal, Carbohydrates: 29g, Fat: 7.5g, Protein: 17g.

27. Avocado and Mango Salad

Preparation time: 15 minutes
Servings: 4

Ingredient:

- 2 romaine hearts, chopped
- 1 cucumber, peeled and cut into ¼-inch cubes
- 2 ripe mangoes, cut into ½-inch cubes
- 2 spring onions, thinly sliced
- 1 large ripe avocado
- 1 cup creamy coconut herb sauce

Preparation:

1. Mix the romaine lettuce, cucumbers, mangoes, scallions, and avocado in a large bowl that can be used for serving.
2. The fruit and vegetables should be drizzled with the Creamy Coconut-Herb Dressing. Mix thoroughly by tossing.

Nutritional value Calories: 253, Fat: 13g, Carbohydrates: 37g, Protein: 4g.

28. Chopped Mediterranean Salad

Preparation time: 15 minutes
Servings: 4

Ingredient:

- 2 cups packed spinach
- 3 large diced tomatoes
- 1 bunch of thinly sliced radishes
- 1 English cucumber, peeled and diced
- 2 spring onions, sliced
- 2 garlic cloves, minced
- 1 tbsp minced fresh mint
- 1 tbsp minced fresh parsley
- 1 cup unsweetened natural almond yogurt
- ¼ cup extra virgin olive oil
- 3 tbsp freshly squeezed lemon juice
- 1 tbsp apple cider vinegar
- ¼ tsp freshly ground black pepper

Preparation:

1. Mix the large amounts of spinach, tomatoes, radishes, cucumber, scallions, garlic, mint, parsley, yogurt, olive oil, lemon juice, cider vinegar, and pepper bowl until everything is evenly distributed. Mix thoroughly by tossing.
2. Add some cooked chicken or fish to this salad to turn it into an entree salad suitable for the Paleo or Mediterranean Action Plans.
3. If you are following the Mediterranean Diet, sprinkle a crumbled goat cheese topping of 3 ounces.

Nutritional value Calories: 194, Fat: 14g, Carbohydrates: 15g, Protein: 4g.

29. Turmeric Chicken Salad

Preparation time: 15 minutes
Cooking time: 20 minutes
Servings: 4

Ingredient:

- 4 boneless and skinless chicken breasts
- 1 tbsp extra virgin olive oil
- 1 tbsp chopped fresh coriander
- 1 garlic clove, minced
- ¼ tsp ground turmeric
- ¼ tsp freshly ground black pepper
- ½ cup unsweetened almond yogurt
- 1 tbsp freshly squeezed lemon juice
- 1 tsp lemon zest
- ½ cup chopped almonds
- 6 cups chopped romaine lettuce

Preparation:

1. Place the chicken breasts in a baking dish on the shallower side.
2. Olive oil, cilantro, garlic, turmeric, and black pepper should be mixed in a small bowl using a whisk. Applying the mixture to the chicken in a uniform manner. Marinate the chicken, covered, in the refrigerator for at least half an hour or for as long as a full day.
3. Prepare the oven to 375 °F. After the oven has been preheated, the baking dish containing the chicken should be placed inside the oven, and the chicken should be baked for twenty minutes. Take the dish out of the oven and set it aside.
4. Combine the yogurt, lemon juice, and zest in a large bowl and whisk together until smooth.
5. After adding the almonds and romaine lettuce, toss everything together so that the lettuce is evenly coated in the dressing.
6. Place the salad on a platter that is suitable for serving. After slicing the chicken breasts into strips, arrange them in a decorative pattern on top of the lettuce.

Nutritional value Calories: 418, Fat: 21g, Carbohydrates: 10 Protein: 46g.

30. Fruit Salad with Poppy Seed Yogurt

Preparation time: 10 minutes
Servings: 4

Ingredients:

For the fruit salad

- 1 baby pineapple - peel and cut into bite-sized pieces
- 1 small Galia melon - cut in half, cut out balls with a Parisian spoon
- 1 organic orange - peel and cut into bite-sized pieces
- 1 apple - wash and cut into bite-sized pieces
- 2 passion fruits - scrape out the pulp, including the seeds, with a spoon
- ½ pomegranate - scrape out the stones with a spoon
- 10 mint leaves - finely cut + 4 tips for decoration

For the poppy seed yogurt

- 5 oz soy yogurt (e.g. from Soyana)
- 2 tbsp poppy seeds
- 1 tsp organic orange zest
- ¼ tsp vanilla powder
- 1 pinch of cardamom powder

Preparation:

1. Mix all the ingredients - except the passion fruit - in a bowl for the fruit salad.
2. Mix all the ingredients in a small bowl for the poppy seed yogurt.
3. Divide the fruit salad into 4 bowls, top with the poppy seed yogurt, then the passion fruit, and enjoy garnished with the mint tips.

Nutritional value Calories: 306, Carbohydrates: 17g, Protein: 11g, Fat: 23g.

31. Alkaline Spring Salad

Preparation time: 30 minutes
Servings: 4

Ingredient:

- 4 cups of approved seasonal greens of your choice (wild arugula, dandelion greens, watercress)
- 1 cup cherry tomatoes
- 1/4 cup walnuts
- 1/4 cup of approved herbs (dill, sweet basil, etc.)

For the dressing:

- 3-4 limes
- 1 tbsp of raw sesame "tahini" butter and cayenne pepper, to taste

Preparation:

1. The main limes should be juiced.
2. Mix the lime juice and "tahini" oil in a small bowl. Try it with cayenne pepper.
3. Cut the cherry tomatoes in half.
4. In a large tub, combine the vegetables, cherry tomatoes, and herbs. Massage the dressing with your hands.
5. Allow the greens to absorb the dressing. Season with additional cayenne pepper, and herbs if desired. Enjoy! Enjoy!

Nutritional value Calories: 242, Fat: 11g, Carbohydrates: 33g, Protein: 7g.

POULTRY AND MEAT RECIPES

32. Lentil-Lamb Ragu

Preparation time: 10 minutes
Cooking time: 30 minutes
Servings: 4

Ingredient:

- 2 tbsp of extra virgin olive oil
- 1 red onion, chopped
- 4 garlic cloves, minced
- 1 pound lean ground lamb
- 1 (14 oz) can of diced tomatoes
- 1 cup chicken broth, plus additional as needed
- ½ cup green lentils
- 1 tsp dried oregano
- 1 tsp ground cumin
- ½ tsp freshly ground black pepper

Preparation:

1. Olive oil should be heated in a large saucepan set over high heat. Sauté the onion for three minutes after adding it to the pan. Sauté the garlic for one minute after adding it to the pan.
2. After breaking up the ground lamb with a spoon, add it to the mixture. Continue to cook for three to four minutes, or until the lamb is browned.
3. Mix in the diced tomatoes, chicken broth, lentils, oregano, and cumin. Simmer for twenty minutes, or until the lentils have reached the desired doneness and the majority of the liquid has been absorbed. If the lentils have not yet become softened but most of the liquid has been absorbed, mix in a little bit of additional broth or some water.

Nutritional value Calories: 402, Fat: 16g, Carbohydrates: 23g, Protein: 41g.

33. Spicy Chicken Drumsticks

Preparation time: 10 minutes
Cooking time: 35 to 45 minutes
Servings: 6

Ingredient:

- 6 chicken drumsticks
- 1 cup unsweetened coconut yogurt
- ½ cup extra virgin olive oil
- 2 limes
- 2 garlic cloves, crushed
- 1 tbsp of raw honey
- 1 tsp ground cumin
- ½ tsp of paprika
- ½ tsp ground turmeric
- ¼ tsp freshly ground black pepper
- Olive oil spray

Preparation:

1. Arrange the chicken in a baking dish that is on the shallow side.
2. To make a smooth sauce, combine the yogurt, olive oil, lime juice, garlic, honey, cumin, paprika, turmeric, and pepper in a small bowl and whisk until combined.
3. The chicken should be topped with the yogurt mixture. Wrap in plastic wrap and place in the refrigerator for at least 30 minutes or overnight.
4. Prepare the oven to 375 °F.
5. Prepare an aluminum foil-lined baking sheet with a rim and lightly grease the foil with nonstick cooking spray.
6. Take the drumsticks out of the marinade and place them on the baking sheet that has been prepared. Put the marinade in the trash.
7. Drumsticks should be baked on the sheet in an oven preheated to 375 °F for 25 to 35 minutes, or until they begin to brown and are cooked through.

Nutritional value Calories: 380, Fat: 31g, Carbohydrates: 9g, Protein: 19g.

34. Lamb Chops with Mustard and Garlic

Preparation time: 30 minutes
Cooking time: 20 minutes
Servings: 4

Ingredient:

- 8 lamb loin chops (4 to 5 oz)
- 2 tbsp chopped fresh oregano
- 4 garlic cloves, minced
- ¼ cup extra virgin olive oil
- 1 tsp Dijon mustard
- ¼ tsp freshly ground black pepper

Preparation:

1. Put the lamb chops in a baking dish on the shallower side.
2. Oregano, garlic, olive oil, Dijon mustard, and pepper should be mixed in a small bowl using a whisk.
3. Lamb chops should be rubbed with the mixture before cooking. Marinate the chops at room temperature for half an hour with the sauce while the dish is covered with plastic wrap.
4. Prepare the oven to 425 °F.
5. Please remove the plastic wrap and put the dish in the oven after it has been preheated. Cook the lamb chops in the oven for 15 to 20 minutes, or until they have a browned crust and are sizzling.
6. Before serving, let the chops sit at room temperature for five minutes.

Nutritional value Calories: 648, Fat: 34g, Carbohydrates: 3g, Protein: 80g.

35. Roasted Chicken Wraps

Preparation time: 5 minutes
Cooking time: 5 minutes
Servings: 4

Ingredient:

- ½ cup low-fat or reduced-fat mayonnaise
- 2 tbsp pickle juice
- 1 tsp freshly ground black pepper
- 1 ½ cups chopped red cabbage
- 1 tbsp apple cider vinegar
- ¼ tsp cayenne pepper
- 1 whole cold roast chicken
- 6 units of wheat, whole wheat, or mixed grain bread

Preparation:

1. Mix the pickle juice, ground black pepper, and mayonnaise in a bowl. Place the mixture in the refrigerator so that it can chill while you make preparations.
2. While that is happening, vinegar, cabbage, and cayenne pepper into a different mixing bowl. To combine the cabbage with the other components, give it a good toss.
3. To prepare the shredded roasted chicken, remove the skin and bones from the chicken and shred the meat into small pieces.
4. Combine the chicken with the mayonnaise mixture after adding it to the chicken.
5. Roll the flatbread slices tightly after the cabbage and chicken have been evenly distributed across the slices.
6. You can either consume it on its own or reheat it in a conventional oven, a microwave oven, or a toaster oven.

Nutritional value Calories: 286, Fat: 8.2g, Protein: 80g.

36. Quick Chicken Stir-Fry

Preparation time: 20 minutes
Cooking time: 20 minutes
Servings: 2

Ingredient:

- 1 ½ tsp olive oil
- 2 cups broccoli florets
- ¾ cup chopped onion
- ¾ cup snow peas
- 1 clove garlic, pressed
- 3 oz boneless chicken breast cut into small pieces
- ¼ cup chickpeas, low sodium, rinsed and drained
- ¼ cup parsley

Preparation:

1. Heat one teaspoon of olive oil in the wok to medium temperature.
2. Stir fry the vegetables for about two minutes, or until they are defrosted and hot, depending on which comes first. Take the vegetables out, place them in a bowl, and set them aside. Start heating the remaining oil in the wok.
3. After pressing one clove of garlic into the hot oil, add the chicken and stir-fry it for about four minutes, or until it is cooked through.
4. After cooking the vegetables and garbanzo beans, place them back into the wok. Continue to toss everything together for an additional two minutes. To accompany the meal, pass some salsa at the table.

Nutritional value Calories: 343, Carbohydrates: 29g, Protein: 26g, Fat: 13g.

37. Barbecue Chicken Salad

Preparation time: 20 minutes
Cooking time: 20 minutes
Servings: 1

Ingredient:

- 2 tsp olive oil
- 3 oz boneless chicken breast, diced
- 1 ½ cups bell peppers, strips
- ¼ cup diced onions
- 1/8 tsp cider vinegar
- 1/8 tsp Worcestershire sauce
- 1 tsp minced garlic
- ½ cup zoned barbecue sauce
- 3 cups lettuce
- 2 cups shredded cabbage
- Pepper to taste

Preparation:

1. Place the chicken breasts, oil, pepper, vinegar, onion, garlic, and Worcestershire sauce in a saute pan. Saute over medium heat until the chicken is cooked through. After browning the chicken and making sure the vegetables are cooked through, add some Zoned barbecue sauce and continue cooking.
2. Keep the lid on the pan and let it simmer for about five minutes, or until it reaches the desired temperature, stirring it every so often to ensure the flavors can combine successfully.
3. Combine the shredded cabbage and the lettuce in a bowl, and then place the salad-cabbage mixture on an oval plate that is quite large. Place the chicken and the vegetable mixture in the middle of the plate. Place the salad cabbage mixture underneath the chicken and vegetable mixture.
4. After giving the dish a light dusting of pepper, serve it as soon as possible.

Nutritional value Calories: 371, Carbohydrates: 50g, Protein: 22g, Fat: 10g.

38. Almond Chicken

Preparation: 10 minutes
Cooking time: 19 minutes
Servings: 4

Ingredient:

- 3 oz boneless chicken breast, sliced
- 2 cups steamed broccoli florets
- 1 ½ tsp olive oil
- 1 pc chopped green pepper
- 1 pc chopped red bell pepper
- ¾ cup chopped onion
- 1 clove chopped garlic
- 1 cup cherry tomatoes, halved
- Pepper to taste
- 2 tsp sliced almonds

Preparation:

1. The broccoli should be steamed. While that happens, bring some olive oil to a simmer in a saute pan.
2. Place the chicken, red and green peppers, garlic, and onion in the pan and saute over medium heat until the chicken is cooked and the vegetables are cooked to a firm but still slightly chewy consistency.
3. Add the steamed broccoli and chopped tomatoes to the pan. Sprinkle some almonds on top.

Nutritional value Calories: 360, Carbohydrates: 45g, Protein: 22g, Fat: 10g.

39. Roasted Chicken with Lemon and Sage

Preparation time: 30 min
Cooking time: 1 hour and 20 minutes
Servings: 4

Ingredient:

- 2 lemons, thinly sliced
- 6 fresh sage leaves
- 1 (6 pounds) chicken
- 3 tsp olive oil, divided
- ¾ pound parsnips, peeled and trimmed
- ¾ pound carrots, peeled and trimmed
- ½ pound turnips, peeled and trimmed
- 1 pound fingerling potatoes, halved
- 2 tbsp chopped fresh thyme

Preparation:

1. Prepare the oven to 425 °F. Under the skin of the chicken, tuck six lemon slices and a few sage leaves. Place the remainder of the lemon in the cavity. Twine the legs together, and tuck the wings underneath the body. Chicken should have 1 teaspoon of oil brushed on it. Put the chicken in a roasting pan, then roast it in the lower third of the oven for about an hour and fifteen minutes, or until an instant-read thermometer registers 165 °F. Place the cooked chicken on a cutting board, and allow it to rest for 15 minutes.
2. Matchstick-size pieces should be cut from the root vegetables. Place potatoes in a baking dish and toss with the remaining oil and thyme. Bake until potatoes are tender. Roast for forty-five minutes, stirring the pan occasionally, or until the vegetables is tender.
3. Remove skin from chicken. Lemons should be thrown away from the cavity. You should cut up enough chicken to serve four people, such as breasts, and serve it with half of the vegetables.

Nutritional value Calories: 380, Carbohydrates: 50g, Protein: 25g, Fat: 12g.

40. Chicken and Vegetable Skewers

Preparation time: 5 minutes
Cooking time: 10 minutes
Servings: 4

Ingredients:

- 1 lb 2 oz large chicken breast fillet (2 large chicken breast fillets)
- 3 onions
- 2 branches rosemary
- 2 branches thyme
- 1 big lemon
- Pepper from the mill
- 1 tbsp olive oil
- 1 lb 8 oz kefir
- 12 oz yoghurt (1.5% fat)
- 2 tbsp cooking cream (15% fat)
- 1 tsp honey
- 2 tsp ground cumin
- 2 fresh mint
- 1 bunch of spring onions
- 1 large yellow pepper
- 16 small cherry tomatoes

Preparation:

1. Rinse, pat dry, dice the chicken breast fillets, and place in a bowl.
2. Peel the onions, dice them very finely and mix them with the poultry.
3. Wash herbs and shake dry. Strip off rosemary needles and chop finely. Also, wipe off the thyme leaves. Halve and squeeze the lemon. Mix the rosemary, thyme, lemon juice, and oil into the poultry cubes. Pepper to taste.
4. Pour the kefir over everything, mix well and cover with cling film. Let it steep (marinate) in the refrigerator for at least 5 hours, preferably overnight.
5. For the dip, stir the yogurt with the cooking cream, honey, and cumin in a small bowl until smooth. Pepper to taste

6. Wash the mint, shake it dry, pluck off the leaves and put some of them aside. Cut the rest into fine strips. Stir into the yogurt mixture and let it steep in the refrigerator for about 1–2 hours.

7. Clean and wash the spring onions and cut them across into pieces about 2 cm long.

8. Halve, core, and wash the pepper and cut it into 2 cm cubes. Wash and drain the cherry tomatoes.

9. Remove the chicken cubes from the marinade and allow draining. Stick them alternately on long kebab skewers with peppers, spring onions, and tomatoes.

10. Grill on all sides for 12-15 minutes, brushing with a little marinade several times in between. Garnish the yogurt dip with the remaining mint leaves and serve with the skewers.

Nutritional value Calories: 370, Carbohydrates: 48g, Protein: 23g, Fat: 11g.

41. Chicken with Mustard and Honey

Preparation time: 10 minutes
Cooking time: 25 minutes
Servings: 4

Ingredient:

- ¼ to 1/3 cup plain Dijon mustard
- ¼ to 1/3 cup honey
- 1 tbsp olive oil
- 2-3 pounds of chicken thighs (or legs)
- 2 sprigs of rosemary (or a generous pinch of dried rosemary)
- Freshly ground black pepper

Preparation:

1. Turn the oven up to 350 °F. Mustard, honey, and olive oil should be mixed in a medium bowl using a whisk. Season with mustard to taste until the dish reaches the level of flavor you desire.
2. Then place the pieces, skin-side up, in a casserole dish on the shallow side. The honey mustard sauce should be spooned over the chicken. Stuff the sprigs of rosemary into the spaces in between the chicken pieces.
3. Bake the thighs for 45 minutes, until a meat thermometer inserted into one of the thighs registers 175 °F, or until the juices that run out of the meat when it is pierced with a knife are clear. Take the casserole dish out of the oven and use a spoon to remove any excess chicken fat rendered over the cooking.
4. Before serving, crack some freshly ground black pepper over the chicken and sprinkle with some black pepper.

Nutritional value Calories: 273, Carbohydrates: 19g, Protein: 25g, Fat: 11g.

42. Chicken Skewers with Mint Sauce

Preparation time: 20 minutes
Cooking time: 20 minutes
Servings: 4

Ingredient:

For mint sauce

- 1 group of fresh mint, steamed
- ½ cup extra virgin olive oil
- 1 clove of Garlic
- 2 tsp of lemon zest
- Tighten the ground black pepper on time

Chicken

- 6 boned skinless chicken breasts, cut into cubes 1 to 2 to 2 inches
- ¼ cup extra virgin olive oil
- ¼ cup lemon juice squeezed
- ¼ tsp of black pepper
- ½ tsp ground turmeric
- 2 branches of fresh mint

Preparation:

To make the mint sauce

1. Combine the mint, olive oil, garlic, lemon zest, and pepper in a blender or food processor. Blend until completely smooth.
2. Refrigerate for no more than four or five days in an airtight container.

To make the chicken

1. To prevent the wooden skewers from catching fire while cooking on the grill, you should first soak them in water for at least half an hour.

2. Place the chicken, olive oil, lemon juice, pepper, turmeric, and mint in a large plastic bag with a zip-top closure. Mix well. Marinate the meat for at least half an hour and up to a day by sealing the bag, placing it in the refrigerator, turning it to coat it, and letting it sit there.
3. Prepare the grill for high heat, or place a stovetop grill over a high heat setting.
4. Place three to four chicken cubes on each skewer. Throw away the marinade and the sprigs of mint.
5. Adjust the temperature of the grill to medium. Cook the chicken over the grill for 15 to 20 minutes, turning the skewers occasionally until each piece of chicken is browned on both sides and is fully cooked through.
6. Serve with the accompanying mint sauce.

Nutritional value Calories: 657, Fat: 51g, Carbohydrates: 2g, Protein: 50g.

43. Chicken with spices

Preparation time: 10 minutes
Cooking time: 45 minutes
Servings: 6

Ingredient:

- 1 whole chicken, cut into 8 pieces
- 1 brown rice flour or coconut flour
- 1 tsp of cumin
- 2 Sweet tsp Paprica
- ½ tsp of garlic powder
- ½ tsp of black pepper
- ½ cup apple juice

Preparation:

1. Prepare the oven to 375 °F.
2. The chicken pieces should be placed in a baking dish.
3. Brown rice flour, cumin, paprika, garlic powder, and black pepper should be mixed in a small bowl. The chicken pieces should be rubbed with the spice mixture.
4. Avoid removing the spice mixture on the chicken as you slowly pour the apple juice into the pan.
5. Put the pan in an oven that has been preheated and bake it for thirty-five to forty-five minutes, or until the chicken is cooked through and has a golden brown color.

Nutritional value Calories: 375, Fat: 21g, Carbohydrates: 10g, Protein: 39g.

44. Chicken Curry

Preparation time: 10 minutes
Cooking time: 45 minutes
Servings: 6

Ingredient:

- 1 tbsp slow-coo ghee
- 3 pounds of boned skinless chicken thighs
- 2 Onions, chopped
- 2 clove -of -Alho, Slély Thin
- 2 tsp of chopped fresh ginger
- 1 tsp curry powder
- 1 tsp of coriander
- 1 tsp of cumin
- 2 cups of chicken broth
- 1 cup of coconut milk
- ¼ cup fresh coriander leaves

Preparation:

1. Put the ghee, chicken, onions, garlic, ginger, curry powder, coriander, cumin, chicken broth, and coconut milk into the slow cooker and mix well. Cook on high for four hours with the lid on.
2. Add the cilantro at the very last minute, before serving.

Nutritional value Calories: 380, Fat: 22g, Carbohydrates: 12g, Protein: 38g.

45. Coconut Chicken

Preparation time: 10 minutes
Cooking time: 45 minutes
Servings: 6

Ingredient:

- 1 table of coconut oil
- 6-skin chicken thighs
- 1 onion, sliced
- 2 clove of garlic, crushed
- 2 tsp of powdered curry
- ¼ tsp of black pepper
- 1 (13.5 oz) can of coconut milk
- 3 cups of chicken broth
- ¼ cup chopped fresh coriander
- 2 chives, sliced
- Pepper

Preparation.

1. Apply a coconut oil coating all over the slow cooker's inside.
2. The chicken, onion, garlic, curry powder, pepper, chicken broth, and coconut milk should all be added at this point. Turn the slow cooker up to high, cover it, and cook for 6 hours.
3. Before serving, top each portion with some chopped cilantro and scallions.

Nutritional value Calories: 400, Fat: 28g, Carbohydrates: 15g, Protein: 40g.

FISH AND SEAFOOD RECIPES

46. Sautéed Shrimp

Preparation time: 10 minutes
Cooking time: 15 minutes
Servings: 4

Ingredient:

- ¼ Extra Virgin Oil
- 1 onion, finely stung
- 1 red pepper, chopped
- 1 ½ pounds of shrimp, peeled and tails removed
- 6 Clove -de -Alho, chopped
- 2 lemon juice
- 2 lemons
- ⅛ tsp of black pepper

Preparation:

1. Olive oil should be heated in a large nonstick skillet over medium-high heat until it shimmers before being added to the pan.
2. Mix in the chopped onion and the roasted red pepper. Cook for approximately six minutes, stirring the mixture occasionally until it is soft.
3. After adding the shrimp, cook them for about 5 minutes, or until they turn pink.
4. Mix in the minced garlic. Cook for another 30 seconds while stirring all the time.
5. Lemon juice, and zest will be added to the dish. Simmer for 3 minutes.

Nutritional value Calories: 345, Fat: 16, Carbohydrates: 10g, Protein: 40g.

47. Shrimp with Spicy Spinach

Preparation time: 10 minutes
Cooking time: 15 minutes
Servings: 4

Ingredient:

- ¼ cup of extra virgin olive oil, divided
- 40 shelled shrimp
- 4 cups of fresh spinach
- 6 cloves of garlic
- ½ cup of freshly pressed orange juice
- 1 tbsp of Sriracha sauce
- ⅛ tsp of freshly ground black pepper

Preparation

1. Two tablespoons of olive oil should be heated until they shimmer in a nonstick skillet and set over medium-high heat.
2. Cook the shrimp in the pan for about four minutes, stirring the pan occasionally until the shrimp turns pink. Place the shrimp on a plate, cover it with aluminum foil to prevent them from drying out, and set aside.
3. Place the skillet back over the heat and wait for the remaining 2 tablespoons of olive oil to reach the point where it shimmers.
4. The spinach should be added. Cook for three minutes while stirring constantly.
5. Mix in the minced garlic. Cook for another 30 seconds while stirring all the time.
6. Orange juice, Sriracha, and black pepper should be mixed in a small bowl. After adding this, continue to cook the spinach for another three minutes. Please serve the shrimp with some spinach.

Nutritional value Calories: 317, Fat: 16, Carbohydrates: 7g, Protein: 38g.

48. Shrimp with Cinnamon Sauce

Preparation time: 10 minutes
Cooking time: 10 minutes
Servings: 4

Ingredient:

- 2 extra virgin olive oil tables
- 40 shelled shrimp
- 2 tbsp of Dijon mustard
- 1 cup of chicken broth without adding salt
- 1 tsp of ground cinnamon
- 1 tsp of onion powder
- ¼ tsp of freshly ground black pepper

Preparation:

1. Olive oil should be heated in a large nonstick skillet over medium-high heat until it shimmers before being added to the pan.
2. Add the shrimp and Cook for about four minutes, stirring the pan occasionally, until it becomes opaque.
3. Mustard, chicken broth, cinnamon, onion powder, and pepper should be mixed in a small bowl using a whisk. Transfer this to the skillet, and cook it over medium heat for another three minutes, stirring the mixture occasionally.

Nutritional value Calories: 315, Fat: 14, Carbohydrates: 7g, Protein: 37g.

49. Salmon and Roasted Asparagus

Preparation time: 5 minutes
Cooking time: 15 minutes
Servings: 4

Ingredient:

- 1 pound of the asparagus spear, cut
- 2 tbsp of extra virgin olive oil
- 1½ pound salmon, cut into four fillets
- ⅛ tsp of freshly cracked black pepper
- Shell and slices of 1 lemon

Preparation:

1. Prepare the oven to 425 °F.
2. Olive oil should be tossed with the asparagus before serving. The bottom of a roasting pan should be covered with a single layer of the mixture.
3. Pepper should be used to season salmon.
4. Place the meat so that the skin is facing down on top of the asparagus.
5. Lemon zest should be sprinkled over the salmon and asparagus, and lemon slices should be placed on top of the fish.
6. Cook for 12 to 15 minutes in an oven that has been preheated, or until the flesh becomes opaque.

Nutritional value Calories: 416, Fat: 26, Protein: 40g.

50. Whitefish Curry

Preparation time: 5 minutes
Cooking time: 15 minutes
Servings: 4

Ingredient:

- 2 tbsp of coconut oil
- 1 onion, chopped
- 2 cloves of garlic, chopped
- 1 tbsp hacked fresh ginger
- 2 tsp of curry powder
- ¼ tsp of freshly ground black pepper
- 1 (4-inch) piece of lemongrass (only white part), squashed with the back of a knife 2 cups cuddled
- 2 cups of chopped broccoli
- 1 (13.5 on) can coconut milk coconut milk
- 1 cup of vegetable broth or chicken broth
- 1 pound of solid white fish fillets
- ¼ cup of chopped fresh coriander
- 1 shallot, thinly cut
- Lemon wedges for garnish

Preparation:

1. The coconut oil should be melted in a large pot over medium-high heat. The onion, garlic, ginger, curry powder, and pepper should all be added at this point. Sauté for 5 minutes.
2. Include broccoli, butternut squash, and lemongrass in the dish. Sauté for 2 minutes more.
3. After stirring in the vegetable broth and coconut milk, bring the mixture to a boil. After lowering the temperature to a simmer, add the fish. Cover the pot and place it over medium-low heat. Simmer for five minutes, or until the fish is completely cooked. Take the lemongrass out of the container and throw it away.

4. Transfer the curry to a serving bowl using a ladle. Serve with lemon wedges and garnish with cilantro and scallion before serving.

Nutritional value Calories: 553, Fat: 39g, Carbohydrates: 22g, Protein: 34g.

51. Whitefish with Spice Removal

Preparation time: 5 minutes
Cooking time: 15 minutes
Servings: 4

Ingredient:

- 2 tbsp of slower cooker ghee, melted, shared
- 4 (6-on) Whitefish fillets
- 1 tbsp of paprika
- 2 sp of bubble
- 2 tsp onion powder
- ½ tsp ground turmeric
- ½ tsp of freshly ground black pepper
- 1 tsp of coconut sugar (optional)

Preparation:

1. Turn the oven up to 400 °F.
2. Spread one tablespoon of ghee in the bottom of a shallow baking dish.
3. After placing the fish fillets in the dish, brush them with one tablespoon of ghee left.
4. Paprika, cumin, onion powder, turmeric, black pepper, and coconut sugar should be mixed in a small bowl (if using).
5. The fillets should be rubbed with one tablespoon of the spice rub, and you should ensure that the rub covers the entire surface of the fish. Keep the leftover rub in a container for later use.
6. The fish should be baked in the oven for 12 to 15 minutes, or until it is firm and cooked through after the baking dish has been placed in a preheated oven.

Nutritional value Calories: 364, Fat: 20g, Carbohydrates: 3g, Protein: 42g.

52. Pecan-Crusted Trout

Preparation time: 15 minutes
Cooking time: 15 minutes
Servings: 4

Ingredient:

- Extra virgin olive oil to brush
- 4 large bone trout fillets
- Freshly ground black pepper
- 1 cup of pecans, finely ground, shared
- 1 tbsp of coconut oil, melted, shared
- 2 tbsp of chopped fresh thyme leaves
- Lemon wedges for garnish

Preparation:

1. Prepare the oven to 375 °F.
2. Olive oil should be used to brush a rimmed baking sheet.
3. On the baking sheet, arrange the trout fillets with the skin side facing down.
4. Each fillet should have a quarter cup of ground pecans pressed with light pressure.
5. After sprinkling the thyme on the fillets, drizzle the melted coconut oil over the nuts and then continue with the next step.
6. Bake the fish for fifteen minutes in an oven that has been preheated, or until it reaches an internal temperature of 145 °F.

Nutritional value Calories: 672, Fat: 59g, Carbohydrates: 13, Protein: 30g.

53. Salmon with Basil Gremolata

Preparation time: 10 minutes
Cooking time: 20 minutes
Servings: 4

Ingredient:

- 4 (5-ounce) skin-on salmon fillets 1 tbsp plus
- 2 tsp extra-virgin olive oil, divided
- ¼ cup freshly squeezed lemon juice
- ¼ tsp freshly ground black pepper, plus additional for seasoning 1 bunch basil
- 1 clove of garlic
- 1 tbsp lemon zest
- 1 (8-ounce) bag of mixed greens
- 1 small cucumber, halved lengthwise and sliced thin
- 1 cup sprouts (radish, onion, or sunflower)

Preparation:

1. Prepare the oven to 375 °F.
2. Place the salmon fillets in a baking dish on the shallower side, and then brush them with two teaspoons of olive oil.
3. Mix in the juice from the lemon. Season with one teaspoon of ground pepper.
4. After placing the dish in an oven that has been preheated, bake the fillets for approximately twenty minutes, or until they are firm and cooked all the way through.
5. The basil, garlic, and lemon zest should be mixed in a food processor. Continue to process until a coarse chop result.
6. Place the sprouts, cucumber, and greens in an attractive arrangement on a serving platter. Sprinkle the greens with pepper and drizzle them with the two tablespoons of olive oil left in the bottle. The salmon fillets should be placed on top of the greens, and the gremolata should be spooned over the salmon.

Nutritional value Calories: 274, Fat: 12g, Carbohydrates: 11g, Protein: 32g.

54. Swordfish with Pineapple and Coriander

Preparation time: 15 minutes
Cooking time: 20 minutes
Servings: 4

Ingredient:

- 1 tbsp of coconut oil
- 2 pounds of swordfish or other firm white fish, cut into 2 -inch pieces 1 cup of fresh pineapple blocks
- ¼ cup of chopped fresh coriander
- 2 tbsp of chopped fresh parsley
- 2 cloves of garlic, chopped
- 1 tbsp of amino coconut
- ¼ tsp of just ground black pepper

Preparation:

1. Turn the oven up to 400 °F.
2. Coconut oil should be used to grease a baking dish before using it.
3. Add the dish's swordfish and pineapple, cilantro, parsley, garlic, coconut aminos, and seasonings of your choice. Combine the components in a slow, even motion.
4. After the oven has been preheated, place the dish and bake for fifteen to twenty minutes, or until the fish is firm when touched. To be served hot.

Nutritional value Calories: 260, Fat: 10g, Carbohydrates: 10g, Protein: 28g.

55. Citrus Salmon on a Bed of Vegetables

Preparation time: 10 minutes
Cooking time: 19 minutes
Servings: 4

Ingredient:

- ¼ cup of extra-virgin oil, divided
- 1½ pounds salmon
- ½ tsp of freshly ground black pepper, divided
- 1 lemon zest
- 6 cups Stemmed and Chopped Swiss Chard
- 3 cloves of garlic, chopped
- 2 lemons juice

Preparation:

1. Two tablespoons of olive oil should be heated until they shimmer in a nonstick skillet and set over medium-high heat.
2. A quarter teaspoon of pepper and lemon zest should be used to season the salmon. When the flesh of the salmon is opaque, it is ready to be removed from the pan after approximately seven minutes of cooking with the skin facing up in the skillet. After you have flipped the salmon, continue cooking it for another three to four minutes. Place on a plate and cover with a tent made of aluminum foil.
3. Place the skillet back over the burner's heat source, add the two additional tablespoons of olive oil, and heat the oil until it shimmers.
4. The Swiss chard should be added. Cook for approximately seven minutes, stirring the mixture occasionally until it is soft.
5. Mix in the minced garlic. Cook for another 30 seconds while stirring all the time.
6. The remaining 14 teaspoons of pepper, and lemon juice should be sprinkled at this point. Prepare for two minutes.
7. On top of the Swiss chard, serve the smoked salmon.

Nutritional value Calories: 363, Total Fat: 25, Carbohydrates: 3g, Protein: 34g.

56. Cevics Salmon

Preparation time: 10 minutes
Servings: 4

Ingredient:

- 1 pound salmon, leather bones, and remove pins, cut into pieces (remove any gray meat)
- ½ cup of newly squeezed lime juice
- 2 tomatoes, diced
- ¼ cup of fresh coriander leaves, chopped
- 1 pepper jalapeño, sown and diced
- 2 tbsp of extra-virgin oil

Preparation:

1. In a medium bowl, combine the lime juice and the salmon and stir to combine. Let it marinate for 20 minutes.
2. Mix in the tomatoes, cilantro, jalapeno, olive oil, until everything combines well.

Nutritional value Calories: 222, Fat: 14g, Carbohydrates: 3g, Protein: 23g.

57. Baked Salmon Steaks

Preparation time: 5 minutes
Cooking time: 15 to 20 minutes
Servings: 4

Ingredient:

- Cooking spray
- 4 (6-ounce) salmon steaks
- 1 tbsp extra-virgin olive oil
- 1 tbsp Spice Rub

Preparation

1. Prepare the oven to 375 °F.
2. Spray a rimmed baking sheet with cooking spray until it is lightly coated.
3. Spread the salmon steaks on the baking sheet and then brush them with olive oil on both sides.
4. Apply the spice rub to both sides of the steaks and grill them.
5. Bake the salmon for 15 to 20 minutes, or until the steaks are firm and cooked through, after placing the baking sheet in a preheated oven.

Nutritional value Calories: 255, Fat: 14g, Carbohydrates: 0g, Protein: 33g.

58. Salmon with Quinoa

Preparation time: 10 minutes
Cooking time: 20 minutes
Servings: 4

Ingredient:

- 1 tbsp extra virgin olive oil, plus extra for brushing
- 1 pound salmon fillets
- Freshly ground black pepper
- 1 red onion, diced
- 2 cups cooked quinoa
- 1 pint cherry tomatoes, halved
- ½ cup chopped fresh basil
- ¼ cup chopped green olives
- 1 tbsp apple cider vinegar

Preparation:

1. Prepare the oven to 375 °F.
2. Olive oil should be used to brush a rimmed baking sheet. After the baking sheet has been prepared, place the salmon fillets on it and brush them with olive oil.
3. Put the sheet into a preheated oven and bake it for twenty minutes.
4. One tablespoon of olive oil should be heated in a large saucepan over medium-high heat. Sauté the onion for three minutes after adding it to the pan.
5. Mix in the quinoa, cherry tomatoes, basil, olives, and cider vinegar until evenly distributed. Continue to cook for one to two minutes, or until the quinoa and tomatoes have reached the desired temperature.
6. Place the tomatoes, quinoa, and salmon on a platter for serving after transferring them to the platter.

Nutritional value Calories: 396, Fat: 16g, Carbohydrates: 36g, Protein: 30g.

59. Salmon Cake with Mango Salsa

Preparation time: 15 minutes
Cooking time: 20 minutes
Servings: 4

Ingredient:

- 2 tbsp coconut oil, melted, divided
- 1 egg
- 2 tsp Dijon mustard
- 1 tsp Worcestershire sauce
- Splash of hot sauce
- 2 spring onions, sliced
- 1½ pounds salmon fillets, cut into 1-inch pieces
- ¼ tsp freshly ground white pepper
- 1 recipe of mango salsa

Preparation:

1. Turn the oven up to 400 °F.
2. Spread one tablespoon of melted coconut oil over a baking sheet's surface with a rim.
3. Mix the egg, the mustard made with Dijon, the Worcestershire sauce, the hot sauce, the scallions, the salmon, and white pepper in a food processor. Put all the ingredients in a food processor and whir them around until the salmon is finely chopped and the mixture can be formed into patties.
4. Form the ingredients into four large patties of approximately the same size.
5. After placing the patties on the baking sheet that has been prepared, use the remaining 1 tablespoon of melted coconut oil to brush them.
6. Put the baking sheet into an oven that has been preheated and bake it for 15 to 20 minutes, or until it has a light brown color and is firm when touched.
7. Serve hot with mango salsa on the side.

Nutritional value Calories: 385, Fat: 19g, Carbohydrates: 20g, Protein: 35g.

60. Salmon with Brown Rice and Spinach

Preparation time: 25 minutes
Cooking time: 30 minutes
Servings: 4

Ingredients:

- Salmon fillets (one piece of salmon about the size of a deck of cards per person)
- Fresh Spinach (I prefer baby spinach) Avocado (1/4-1/2 per person)
- Brown Rice or Quinoa
- For the dressing: Balsamic Vinegar Olive Oil
- Maple Syrup

Preparation

1. Get started on preparing your brown rice or quinoa by following the directions on the package. Both of these dishes are prepared in a rice cooker. This is a fantastic meal we can make with the leftover brown rice or quinoa that we always seem to have to lie around in the refrigerator.

2. Cook your salmon. This is typically The Hubs' area of responsibility. Honey and soy sauce is a tasty combination that we like to use as a basting sauce for the meat. In most cases, the Hubs prepares it on the barbecue with the skin side down for about ten minutes. We also prepare it in our toaster oven by setting the temperature to 350 °F and cooking it for approximately 8 to 12 minutes. The cooking time will vary depending on the salmon portions' size and the salmon's desired doneness; I like my salmon to be slightly undercooked.

3. Get ready to make the salad dressing. Sandy Cooper, a wonderful woman, and a fabulous cook, gave me the recipe for my balsamic dressing. Mix 1 portion of maple syrup, 2 portions of olive oil, and 3 portions of balsamic vinegar. My portions are typically measured in tablespoons, but you could just as easily use teaspoons or cups (1/2 cups, 1/4 cups, etc.) if you wanted to make a lot of food to store in your refrigerator.

4. Prepare your baby spinach by dressing it with balsamic vinegar.

5. After the salmon has finished cooking, peel off the skin and place a portion of the fish on top of each salad. Place some dressed baby spinach on the bottom of each

plate, and then top with avocado cut into individual slices or chunks. Include one measure of quinoa or brown rice in the dish.

6. Serve, and have fun with it!

Nutritional value Calories: 242, Fat: 11g, Carbohydrates: 33g, Protein: 7g.

61. Lemon-Scented Steamed Salmon with Zucchini

Preparation time: 15 minutes
Cooking time: 30 minutes
Servings: 1

Ingredients:

- 1 pc sliced onion
- 1 pc sliced lemon
- 2 pc sliced zucchini
- 1 cup white wine
- 2 cups water
- 4 – 6 oz pieces of Salmon fillets
- ¼ tsp freshly ground pepper

Preparation:

1. Put the lemon, zucchini, onion, water, and wine in the bottom of a large Dutch oven. Cover the ingredients with foil.
2. Pepper should be used to season the salmon fillets.
3. In the meantime, install a steamer rack over the vegetables in the oven and set them to a temperature between medium and high heat. Wait for the liquid to start boiling.
4. After changing the temperature from medium to low, place the fillets on the rack carefully. Steam the fillets for eight to ten minutes, covered, or until they reach an internal temperature of 145 °F.
5. On top of the vegetables that are being served, place the fillets. After adding the liquid from the poaching process, top the dish with sliced olives and a garnish, if desired.

Nutritional value Calories: 251, Carbohydrates: 26g, Protein: 22g, Fat: 6g.

62. Quinoa and Broccoli Stir Fry

Preparation time: 10 minutes
Cooking time: 10 minutes
Servings: 4

Ingredient:

- 1 tbsp coconut oil
- 2 leeks, white part only, sliced
- 2 cloves of garlic, minced
- 4 cups chopped broccolini
- ½ cup vegetable broth, or water
- 1 tsp curry powder
- 2 cups of cooked quinoa
- 1 tbsp coconut aminos

Preparation:

1. The coconut oil should be melted in a large skillet over high heat. Mix in the garlic and the leeks. Sauté for 2 minutes.
2. Include the broccolini in the dish along with the vegetable broth. Cook the meat for 5 minutes with the lid on the pan.
3. Mix in the curry powder, quinoa, and coconut aminos until evenly distributed. Cook the quinoa, uncovered, for two to three minutes, or until it has reached the desired temperature.
4. You can serve it at room temperature as a salad or warm it up as a side dish.

Nutritional value Calories: 251, Carbohydrates: 26g, Protein: 22g, Fat: 6g.

63. Roasted Broccoli and Cashews

Preparation time: 10 minutes
Cooking time: 20 minutes
Servings: 4

Ingredient:

- 6 cups of broccoli florets
- 2 tbsp of extra virgin olive oil
- 1 tbsp coconut aminos
- ½ cup roasted cashews

Preparation:

1. Prepare the oven to 375 °F.
2. Toss the broccoli with olive oil in a large bowl. Place the broccoli in the bowl. Place the broccoli in a single layer on a baking sheet coated with cooking spray. Put the baking sheet into a preheated oven and roast it for fifteen to twenty minutes, or until the broccoli is cooked through.
3. After the broccoli has been roasted, place it in a large bowl with the cashews and coconut aminos, and then serve.

Nutritional value Calories: 209, Fat: 15g, Carbohydrates: 15g, Protein: 6g.

64. Buddha Bowl

Preparation time: 15 minutes
Cooking time: 35 minutes
Servings: 6

Ingredient:

- 1 cup brown basmati rice
- 2 cups of vegetable broth
- 3 tbsp coconut oil, divided
- 1 pint sliced mushrooms
- 2 cloves of garlic, thinly sliced
- 4 oz fresh peas, without strings
- 2 carrots, thinly sliced
- ½ cup frozen peas, thawed
- 2 chives, thinly sliced
- 3 tbsp chopped fresh cilantro
- 3 tbsp freshly squeezed lime juice
- 1 tbsp toasted sesame oil
- 1 tbsp coconut aminos
- ½ tsp red pepper flakes

Preparation:

1. Basmati rice, vegetable broth, and one tablespoon of coconut oil should be combined and stirred in a medium saucepan set over high heat. Bring to a boil, then lower the heat to a simmer for a few minutes. Rice should be cooked with the lid on for 25 to 35 minutes, or until it reaches the desired tenderness.
2. The remaining 2 tablespoons of coconut oil should be melted in a large pan set over high heat. Put the mushrooms in the dish. For about five minutes, or until they have a light browning on them, sauté them.
3. Next, stir in the carrots, snow peas, and garlic. Sauté for 3 minutes more. After the peas have thawed, add them to the pan and cover them so they can finish warming up.

4. After the vegetables have been sautéed, add them to the rice and stir until combined. Stir in the scallions, cilantro, lime juice, sesame oil, coconut aminos, and red pepper flakes.

Nutritional value Calories: 371, Fat: 15g, Carbohydrates: 51g, Protein: 9g.

65. Mushroom Risotto

Preparation time: 15 minutes
Cooking time: 20 minutes
Servings: 4

Ingredient:

- 2 tbsp of extra virgin olive oil
- 1 large shallot, sliced
- 1 clove of garlic, minced
- 1 pint sliced mushrooms
- 1½ cups of arboreal rice
- 3 cups vegetable broth, warmed
- ½ tsp freshly ground black pepper
- A pinch of ground nutmeg
- 1 tbsp chopped fresh thyme leaves
- balsamic vinegar, to decorate

Preparation:

1. Olive oil should be heated in a large skillet set over high heat. To the pan, add the garlic and shallot. Sauté for 3 minutes.
2. Mix in the rice and the mushrooms. Sauté for 3 minutes more.
3. Turn the temperature down to medium-high. When adding the vegetable broth, do so one cup at a time, stirring constantly between each addition, and wait until the rice has absorbed the previous cup's worth of liquid before proceeding with the recipe.
4. After the chicken broth has been completely absorbed, season the chicken with pepper, and nutmeg. Have a taste of the risotto to determine whether or not the rice is fully cooked; it should be chewy but not mushy.
5. Place the risotto in a dish that is suitable for serving. To finish, sprinkle the balsamic vinegar over the thyme leaves and drizzle with some of the vinegar.

Nutritional value Calories: 359, Fat: 9g, Carbohydrates: 60g, Protein: 10g

66. Pad Thai Noodles with Buckwheat

Preparation time: 15 minutes
Cooking time: 15 minutes
Servings: 4

Ingredient:

- 1 (8-ounce) package of buckwheat soba noodles
- 1 tbsp coconut oil
- 1 red onion, chopped
- 2 cloves of garlic, minced
- 2 tsp chopped fresh ginger
- 1 zucchini, chopped
- 2 bok choy, sliced thin
- 1 tbsp coconut aminos
- 1 tbsp apple cider vinegar
- 3 tbsp almond butter or cashew butter
- 2 tbsp toasted sesame oil
- 1 tbsp raw honey or coconut sugar
- ¼ cup vegetable broth without adding salt
- 2 chives, thinly sliced
- ¼ cup chopped fresh cilantro
- 2 tbsp of sesame seeds

Preparation:

1. After cooking the soba noodles following the instructions on the package, drain them and set them aside.
2. The coconut oil should be melted in a large pan over high heat. Sauté for 5 minutes. The red onion, garlic, ginger, zucchini, and bok choy should all be added.
3. The coconut aminos, cider vinegar, almond butter, honey, and vegetable broth should all be added at this point. Continue to stir frequently while cooking for another minute.
4. After adding the soba noodles to the pan and giving them a quick sauté, use a large spatula to move the mixture from the bottom to the top of the pan to combine the

vegetables and the soba noodles. Place the Pad Thai in a dish suitable for serving and to finish, sprinkle with cilantro, scallions, and sesame seeds.

Nutritional value Calories: 486, Fat: 21g, Carbohydrates: 63g, Protein: 19g.

67. Lentils with Tomatoes and Turmeric

Preparation time: 10 minutes
Cooking time: 10 minutes
Servings: 4

Ingredient:

- 2 tbsp of extra virgin olive oil, plus extra for decoration
- 1 onion, finely chopped
- 1 tbsp of ground turmeric
- 1 tsp of garlic powder
- 1 can (14 oz) Lentils, drained
- 1 can (14 oz) of sliced tomatoes, drained
- ¼ tsp of freshly ground black pepper

Preparation:

1. Olive oil should be heated in a large pot over medium-high heat until it shimmers before use.
2. Cook for about five minutes, stirring the mixture occasionally until the onion is soft. Add the turmeric to the pan.
3. Mix in the garlic powder, lentils, tomatoes, and seasonings of your choice, including pepper. Continue to stir occasionally while cooking for another 5 minutes. If desired, serve with a garnish of additional olive oil drizzled on top.

Nutritional value Calories: 420, Fat: 2g, Carbohydrates: 65g, Protein: 27g.

68. Wholemeal Pasta with Tomato Sauce and Basil

Preparation time: 15 minutes
Cooking time: 10 minutes
Servings: 4

Ingredient:

- 2 tbsp of extra virgin olive oil
- 1 onion, minced
- 6 cloves of garlic, minced
- 2 (28 oz) cans of crushed tomatoes, undrained
- ¼ cup basil leaves, sliced
- 1 (8 oz) package of wholemeal pasta

Preparation:

1. Olive oil should be heated in a large pot over medium-high heat until it shimmers before use.
2. Mix in the chopped onion. Cook for approximately five minutes, stirring the mixture occasionally until it is soft.
3. Mix in the minced garlic. Cook for another 30 seconds while stirring all the time.
4. Mix the tomatoes, and raise the heat to a low simmer. Turn the heat down to medium and cook for another 5 minutes, stirring occasionally.
5. Take the pan off the heat and stir in the basil once it has cooled. Combine with the pasta in the bowl.

Nutritional value Calories: 330, Fat: 8g, Carbohydrates: 56g, Protein: 14g.

69. Fried Rice with Cabbage

Preparation time: 10 minutes
Cooking time: 12 minutes
Servings: 4

Ingredient:

- 2 tbsp of extra virgin olive oil
- 8 oz tofu, chopped
- 6 spring onions, white and green parts, thinly sliced
- 2 cups kale, stemmed and chopped
- 3 cups cooked brown rice
- ¼ cup satay sauce

Preparation:

1. Olive oil should be heated in a large skillet over medium-high heat until it shimmers before being used.
2. To the pan, add the kale, tofu, and scallions. Cook for five to seven minutes, stirring the vegetables regularly until they become tender.
3. Put in some brown rice as well as some stir-fry sauce. Cook for three to five minutes, stirring once or twice until the food is completely warmed.

Nutritional value Calories: 301, Fat: 11g, Carbohydrates: 36g, Protein: 16g.

70. One Pot of Tomato Basil Pasta

Preparation time: 5 minutes
Cooking time: 10 minutes
Servings: 4

Ingredient:

- 2 tbsp extra virgin olive oil, plus additional for drizzling
- 1 onion, sliced thin
- 2 cloves of garlic, thinly sliced
- 1 pound of wholemeal penne
- 1 (15-ounce) can of diced tomatoes
- ¼ tsp freshly ground black pepper
- ¼ cup chopped fresh basil, plus 4 whole basil leaves
- 4½ cups of water

Preparation:

1. Two tablespoons of olive oil should be heated in a large Dutch oven with a heavy bottom over medium heat. To that, add the garlic and the onion. To coat with the oil, stir thoroughly.
2. The pasta, tomatoes, four whole basil leaves, and water should all be added to the pot at this point. The liquid should be brought to a boil before the pot is covered. Cook for between eight and ten minutes. Check to see if the pasta is done, and if it isn't, add some more water to the pot. Carry on with the cooking until the pasta reaches the desired tenderness.
3. Place the cooked pasta in a serving bowl, top with the remaining 14 cups of chopped basil, and finish with a drizzle of olive oil.

Nutritional value Calories: 518, Fat: 11g, Carbohydrates: 95g, Protein: 10g.

71. Stir-Fried Tofu and Spinach

Preparation time: 10 minutes
Cooking time: 10 minutes
Servings: 4

Ingredient:

- 2 tbsp extra virgin olive oil
- 1 onion, chopped
- 4 cups of fresh baby spinach
- 8 oz tofu
- 3 cloves of garlic, chopped juice from 1 orange
- 3 tbsp orange juice
- ⅛ tbsp freshly ground black pepper

Preparation:

1. Olive oil should be heated in a large skillet over medium-high heat until it shimmers before being used.
2. Include the onion, baby spinach, and tofu in the dish. Getting the onion to the desired consistency will take about five minutes of cooking time with occasional stirring.
3. Mix in the minced garlic. Cook for another 30 seconds while stirring all the time.
4. Mix in the orange juice, and orange zest. Cook for three minutes while stirring until the food is completely warmed.

Nutritional value Calories: 518, Fat: 11g, Carbohydrates: 95g, Protein: 10g.

72. Low Carb Zucchini Lasagne Vegetarian

Preparation time: 10 minutes
Cooking time: 40 minutes
Servings: 6

Ingredients:

- 800 g frozen spinach
- 1 piece of onion
- 4 cloves of garlic
- 1 can peeled tomatoes
- 2 tsp tomato paste
- 1 pinch of pepper
- 1 handful of fresh basil
- 2 tbsp Parmesan
- 1 pack of mozzarella
- 3 medium zucchinis
- 1 tsp parsley
- 1 tsp oregano
- 3-4 tbsp grated cheese

Preparation:

1. After it has been thawed, the spinach should be squeezed to remove any excess liquid. put him aside.
2. Prepare the onion and garlic by chopping them very finely. They should be cooked in a skillet with olive oil.
3. After peeling the tomatoes, add them along with the tomato paste.
4. Cover the saucepan, reduce the heat to low, and simmer the sauce for 15 minutes.
5. Take the sauce off the heat and stir the herbs in the following order: basil, spinach, oregano, and parsley.
6. Cut the zucchini into thin slices. After drying them off with kitchen paper, arrange them in a single layer on a baking sheet. Put the slices of zucchini in the oven and cook them for five minutes. Remove them from the oven once the food has

absorbed all the liquid. Following these instructions will stop the lasagna from becoming too watery.

7. The tomato sauce is spread out as the first layer. The first layer of zucchini should be placed on top.

8. Next is a layer of mozzarella, which you can see here. And finally, the parmesan cheese.

9. And then there was the tomato sauce and the zucchini. The final layer consists of a sauce made of tomato and spinach. Sprinkle some grated cheese over the top.

10. Bake the lasagna made with zucchini and other vegetables for thirty minutes at 400 °F. After that, cover the dish with parchment paper and continue cooking for another 10 minutes.

11. Ten minutes of standing time should be allowed for the vegetarian low-carb lasagne before it is served.

Nutritional values Calories: 178 kcal, Fat: 11g, Carbohydrates: 95g, Protein: 10g.

73. Low Carb Pizza Crust With Quark

Preparation time: 5 minutes
Cooking time: 30 minutes
Servings: 1

Ingredients:

For the dough

- 2 ½ cottage cheese
- 1 egg
- 2 ½ grated pizza cheese

For covering

- 3 tbsp tomato paste
- 1 handful of arugula
- 7 oz prosciutto

Preparation:

1. Preheat the oven to 360 °F and line a baking tray with paper.
2. Mix the cottage cheese, egg, and cheese in a bowl. You can easily do this with a fork. Or you use a blender.
3. Spread the dough in a round shape on the baking paper.
4. Bake the dough for 10 to 15 minutes.
5. Meanwhile, mix the tomato paste with a little water. Spread the tomato paste on the dough.
6. Bake the pizza for another 15 minutes and then top it with rocket and prosciutto.

Nutritional values Calories: 395 cal, Fat: 31g, Carbohydrates: 9g, Protein: 19g.

SNACKS RECIPES

74. Cucumber Yoghurt Dip

Preparation time: 15 minutes
Servings: 4

Ingredient:

- 1 cucumber, peeled and shredded
- 1 cup plain coconut yogurt
- 1 clove of garlic, minced
- 1 scallion, chopped
- 2 tbsp chopped fresh dill
- 2 tbsp freshly squeezed lemon juice
- 2 tbsp extra virgin olive oil

Preparation:

1. Put the shredded cucumber in a filter with a fine mesh so that any excess liquid can drain out.
2. Combine the yogurt, garlic, scallion, dill, and lemon juice in a small bowl and stir until combined.
3. After the cucumber is drained, fold it and transfer it to a serving bowl.
4. Olive oil should be drizzled over the dish just before it is served.

Nutritional values Calories: 100 cal, Fat: 1g, Carbohydrates: 18g, Protein: 17g.

75. White Bean Dip

Preparation time: 15 minutes
Servings: 4

Ingredient:

- 1 (15 ounce) can of kidney beans, drained and rinsed
- 1 clove of garlic
- 1 tbsp tahini or almond butter
- 3 tbsp extra virgin olive oil
- ¼ cup chopped pitted green olives
- 1 tbsp chopped fresh parsley
- 2 tbsp freshly squeezed lemon juice

Preparation:

1. White beans, garlic, and tahini should all be processed in a food processor. While the machine is operating at a low speed, gradually add the olive oil in a thin stream that remains constant. If the dip is too thick, add a little water to thin it out.
2. Include olives, and parsley in the dish. Pulse to combine. Mix in the juice from the lemon.
3. Place the mixture in a serving bowl, and accompany it with gluten-free crackers and raw vegetables.

Nutritional value Calories: 363, Total Fat: 25, Total Carbs: 3g, Protein: 34g.

76. Creamy Broccoli Dip

Preparation time: 20 minutes
Servings: 5

Ingredient:

- 1 cup broccoli florets
- 1 clove of garlic
- 1 spring onion, roughly chopped
- ¾ cup unsweetened almond yogurt or coconut yogurt
- ½ avocado
- 1 tbsp freshly squeezed lemon juice
- ½ tsp dried dill Pinch of red pepper flakes

Preparation:

1. Put a steamer basket inside a medium-sized pot, fill it with water to a depth of two inches, and then place it over medium-high heat.
2. Put the broccoli in the steamer basket, cover it, and steam it for about five minutes until it turns a vibrant green color. Take the pan off the burner and drain the broccoli while you wait.
3. Place the garlic, scallion, yogurt, avocado, lemon juice, dill, and red pepper flakes in the bowl of a food processor and process until smooth. A few quick pulses should be enough to give the appearance of the mixture is roughly chopped.
4. Add the broccoli, and continue processing until everything is thoroughly combined; the mixture should be chunky, rather than completely puréed. You can serve this dip with sweet potato chips or sticks of fresh vegetables like carrots and celery.

Nutritional value Calories: 82, Fat: 7g, Carbohydrates: 7g, Protein: 1g.

77. Smoked Trout and Mango Wraps

Preparation time: 15 minutes
Servings: 4

Ingredient:

- 4 large green lettuce leaves, thick stems removed
- 4 oz of smoked trout, divided
- 1 cup chopped mango, divided
- 1 leek, sliced, divided
- 2 tbsp freshly squeezed lemon juice, divided

Preparation:

1. Spread the lettuce leaves out in a single layer on a flat surface. Place a piece of trout and some mango on each leaf in equal amounts. The dish is finished with a sprinkling of scallions and a drizzle of lemon juice.
2. Wrap the lettuce leaves up like a burrito and place them on the serving dish with the seam side facing down.

Nutritional value Calories: 108, Fat: 3g, Carbohydrates: 13g, Protein: 9g.

78. Kale Chips

Preparation time: 20 minutes
Cooking time: 20 minutes
Servings: 4

Ingredient:

- 1 bunch kale, thoroughly washed and dried, ribs removed and cut into 2-inch strips
- 2 tbsp extra virgin olive oil

Preparation:

1. Prepare the oven to 275 °F.
2. In a large bowl, use your hands to combine the kale and olive oil until the kale is completely covered in oil and the oil is evenly distributed throughout the kale.
3. Place the kale in a single layer on a baking sheet coated with cooking spray.
4. Bake the kale for approximately twenty minutes, or until it reaches the desired level of crispiness, after placing the baking sheet in a preheated oven. Flip the chips over once they have been in the oven for half the time to ensure that both sides become crisp.
5. Before serving, let the chips come to room temperature.

Nutritional value Calories: 50, Carbohydrates: 2.5g, Protein: 1.5g.

79. Blueberry Nut Student Mix

Preparation time: 5 minutes
Cooking time: 5 minutes
Servings: 4

Ingredient:

- 1 tbsp extra virgin olive oil
- 1 cup almonds
- ½ tsp Chinese five-spice powder
- ½ cup dried blueberries

Preparation:

1. Olive oil should be heated in a large skillet that does not stick to the pan over medium-high heat until it shimmers.
2. After adding the almonds, and Chinese five spices, continue cooking for another two minutes while stirring frequently.
3. Take it off the heat, and allow it to cool. Add the blueberries and stir them in.

Nutritional value Calories: 179, Fat: 16g, Carbohydrates: 8g, Protein: 5g.

80. Guacamole

Preparation time: 10 minutes
Servings: 4

Ingredient:

- 2 avocados, peeled, stoned, and diced
- ½ red onion, chopped
- 2 cloves of garlic, finely chopped juice from 1 lime
- 2 tbsp chopped fresh coriander leaves

Preparation:

1. Mix the avocados, red onion, garlic, lime juice, the cilantro in a medium bowl. To combine everything, give it a quick mash with a fork.

Nutritional value Calories: 215, Fat: 20g, Carbohydrates: 11g, Protein: 2g.

81. Garlic Ranch Dip

Preparation time: 10 minutes
Servings: 4

Ingredient:

- ¼ cup anti-inflammatory mayonnaise
- ¼ cup buttermilk
- 3 cloves of garlic, chopped
- 1 tbsp chopped fresh chives
- 1 tbsp chopped fresh dill
- ¼ tsp freshly ground black pepper

Preparation:

1. Mayonnaise, buttermilk, garlic, chives, dill, and pepper should be mixed in a small bowl before adding the other ingredients.

Nutritional value Calories: 215, Fat: 20g, Carbohydrates: 11g, Protein: 2g.

82. Sauteed Apples and Ginger

Preparation time: 10 minutes
Cooking time: 10 minutes
Servings: 4

Ingredient:

- 2 tbsp coconut oil
- 3 apples, peeled, includes, and sliced
- 1 tsp grated fresh ginger
- 1 tsp. ground cinnamon
- 1 packet of stevia

Preparation:

1. Coconut oil should be heated in a large nonstick skillet over medium-high heat until it shimmers before being used.
2. The apples, ginger, cinnamon, stevia, and should all be added at this point. Cook the apples for seven to ten minutes, stirring the pan occasionally until they are tender.

Nutritional value Calories: 152, Fat: 7g, Carbohydrates: 24g, Protein: 1g.

83. Chickpea Flour Waffle

Preparation time: 20 minutes
Cooking time: 15 minutes
Servings: 8

Ingredient:

- 6 oz chickpea flour
- 1 oz arrowroot
- 1 cup vegetable milk
- 4 tbsp olive oil
- 1 onion
- 1 tbsp sesame seeds
- ½ sachet of yeast
- pepper
- cumin
- coriander

Avocado mousse

- 4 ½ silken tofu
- 2 avocados
- 1 lemon (juice)

Preparation:

1. In a bowl, combine the chickpea flour, arrowroot, baking powder, spices, and sesame seeds, and pepper.
2. Add milk and olive oil. Stir vigorously until you get a smooth paste.
3. Brown the onion in a skillet and add it to the waffle batter. Let stand 30 minutes.
4. Cook in a waffle iron (identical to classic waffles) adding a little oil if necessary.
5. Remove the flesh from the avocados. Mix with the silken tofu and lemon juice.
6. Serve the waffles with a green salad and the avocado mousse.

Nutritional value Calories: 108, Fat: 6g, Carbohydrates: 12g, Protein: 3g.

84. Red Velvet Cake

Preparation time: 20 minutes
Cooking time: 20 minutes
Servings: 12

Ingredients:

- 9 oz buckwheat flour
- 1 lb raw beets
- 1 ½ oz unrefined sugar
- 1 packet of yeast
- 3 eggs
- 1 oz unsweetened cocoa
- 10 tbsp vegetable milk
- 1 tbsp cinnamon
- 2 oz coconut oil
- 1 pomegranate (optional)

Preparation:

- Peel the beets and grate them finely.
- In a salad bowl or the mixer bowl, put the coconut oil in a solid state (room temperature). Add the sugar and beat vigorously to froth.
- Add the eggs one by one. Stir well to obtain a homogeneous mixture.
- Add the cocoa, the flour in which you mixed the yeast, and the cinnamon. Beat well and thin with the milk. Add the finely grated beets.
- Pour into a cake mold or individual mold. Bake at 160°C for 15 to 20 minutes.

Nutritional value Calories: 657, Fat: 51g, Carbohydrates: 2g, Protein: 50g.

85. Root Vegetable Savory Cheesecake

Preparation time: 20 minutes
Servings: 4

Ingredients:

Dough

- 2 oz rice flakes
- 4 oz rolled oats
- 2 oz preferably complete sesame puree
- 6 tsp olive oil
- ¾ oz sesame seeds
- 1 tbsp herbs of Provence

Trim

- 12 oz Greek-style soy yogurt
- ½ cup vegetable milk
- 1 tsp agar agar
- Pepper
- 1 tbsp thyme
- 1 tbsp oregano
- 1 tbsp basil
- 1 beet
- 2 carrots
- 1 parsnip

Preparation:

1. Put all the ingredients for the dough in a blender and mix for 3-4 minutes to form a homogeneous paste. Adjust seasoning.
2. Place a circle of parchment paper in the bottom of a springform pan or a dish if using circles. Divide the mixture into the molds, and press well with a spoon to form a paste about 5 mm thick. Reserve in the refrigerator.

3. Dissolve the agar-agar in the milk in a small saucepan. Boil then transfer to a bowl. Leave to cool for 1 minute then pour in the Greek yogurt. Add pepper and Provencal herbs and whisk the preparation.
4. Take the dough out of the fridge and add the yogurt preparation about 1 cm. Leave to set for at least 2 hours in the refrigerator.
5. When ready to serve, brush the vegetables (peel them if they are not from organic farming). Cut some into thin slices (preferably using a mandolin) and grate the rest.
6. Take the cheesecakes out of the fridge, remove the circle and arrange the vegetable slices on top. Serve immediately with grated vegetables.

Nutritional value Calories 453 Fat: 4g, Carbohydrates: 55g, Protein: 9g.

86. Chocolate Ice Cream

Preparation time: 10 minutes
Servings: 8

Ingredients:

- 1 ¼ cup vegetable milk
- 2 ½ pastry chocolate
- 7 oz coconut cream

Preparation:

1. In a saucepan, melt the chocolate and coconut cream. Remove from the heat and add the milk then refrigerate for at least 2 hours.
2. Simmer for about 30 minutes in the ice cream maker when the mixture is very cold and mold into individual jars. Be careful, depending on the quality of the ice cream maker, the mixture tends to massage very quickly on the edges and block the ice cream maker. You must therefore quickly pour your mixture well into the center.

Nutrition value (per serving) Calories 216 Fat: 11g, Carbohydrates: 28g, Protein: 4g.

FRUITS AND DESSERT RECIPES

87. Delicious Mango Cheesecake

Preparation time: 20 minutes
Servings: 16

Ingredient:

Crust

- 1 cup walnuts
- ¼ cup shredded dehydrated soft jelly coconut
- 1 cup dates

Filling

- 2 cups walnuts (soaked overnight and drained)
- 1/3 cup agave
- 1 lime juice
- 1 cup coconut oil
- 2 large mangoes (peeled and diced)
- 6 tbsp coconut oil
- 1 tbsp lime zest

Preparation:

1. To prepare a baking sheet 8 inches by 8 inches, line it with parchment paper.
2. Combine the walnuts, soft jelly coconut, and dates in a blender. If the dough is not sticky enough, add a few more dates and press it into the bottom of the pan in an even layer. Place it in the freezer for later use.
3. Around three minutes should be spent blending the coconut milk and walnuts until they reach a smooth consistency. After adding the key lime juice and zest, agave syrup, mango cubes, and coconut oil, continue to blend the mixture.
4. After the pan has been prepared, pour the mixture and spread it out evenly.
5. Place in the refrigerator for about 2 hours before serving. Enjoy your meal even when it's frozen solid.

6. **Nutritional value** Calories: 301, Fat: 11g, Carbohydrates: 36g, Protein: 16g.
7.

88. Raw Energy Balls

Preparation time: 15 minutes
Servings: 1

Ingredients:

- ½ cup blueberries
- ½ cup walnuts or Brazil nuts
- ½ cup dried dates
- 2 cups shredded soft jelly coconut
- 1 tbsp agave syrup
- 1 tsp of date sugar

Preparation:

1. The nuts should be ground into a powder.
2. Add the date sugar, dried blueberries, and date pieces to the bowl. Slowly adding the agave syrup will result in the formation of a smooth paste.
3. Chill the mixture for anywhere between 30 and 60 minutes.
4. Using the tablespoon, roll it up to form a ball, and then store it in the freezer for anywhere from one week to three months.

Nutritional value Calories: 356, Fat: 12g, Carbohydrates: 38g, Protein: 25g.

89. Raspberry Chocolate Slices

Preparation time: 30 minutes
Cooking time: 3 hours 10 minutes.
Servings: 6

Ingredient:

- 4 eggs
- 4 oz cane sugar (plus two tbsp sugar for dusting)
- 3 oz pastry flour
- 1 oz cocoa powder
- ¼ cup orange juice (to taste; freshly squeezed)
- 2 tbsp orange liqueur (or two tbsp orange juice)
- 14 oz of raspberries
- 5 tbsp of raspberry jelly
- 1 cup of red grape juice
- 1 pinch of red cake frosting

Preparation:

1. Separate eggs. Using a hand mixer, beat the egg whites until they form stiff peaks.
2. Egg yolks, 100 grams (approximately half a cup) of sugar, and two tablespoons of hot water should be mixed until it forms a creamy consistency.
3. Flour and cocoa should be combined, then sifted. Mixing the beaten egg whites and flour with the egg yolk mixture should be done in alternating order.
4. Put parchment paper on a baking sheet approximately 30 centimeters by 40 centimeters (11 inches by 16 inches). The dough was spread ououncet on the paper. Turn the baked cake upside down onto a cooling rack and let it cool. Bake for 12 minutes on the second rack from the bottom of an oven that has been preheated to 400 °F
5. Take the parchment paper off the top of the cake. Drizzle orange liqueur over the cake. The cake should be sliced lengthwise into three equal strips. After being washed and drained in a sieve, the raspberries should be set aside.
6. Raspberry jelly should be painted onto the surface of the cake slices.

7. Stack the cake slices one atop the other to serve. The raspberries should be placed on top.
8. Prepare the glaze following the instructions on the package, then combine it with the remaining sugar and grape juice. Pour the syrup over the fresh raspberries. After the cake has been chilled for two hours, cut it into slices.

Nutritional values Calories: 335 kcal, Protein: 8g, Fat: 6g, Carbohydrates: 59g.

90. Papaya Mango Smoothie with Apple Juice

Preparation time: 15 minutes
Servings: 4

Ingredients:

- 1 small ripe papaya (about 10 oz)
- 1 small ripe mango
- 1 juicy orange
- ½ cup unfiltered apple juice
- Ice cubes

Preparation:

1. After cutting the papaya in half and scooping out the seeds with a spoon, peel it and cut the flesh into cubes.
2. After peeling the mango, cut the flesh into slices around the pit, then cut the slices into cubes.
3. Orange juice should be squeezed out and blended in the blender with apple juice.

Nutritional values Calories: 230 kcal, Protein: 3g, Fat: 1g, Carbohydrates: 48g.

91. Mango Sorbet with Raspberry Sauce

Preparation time: 20 minutes
Cooking time: 1 hour 30 minutes.
Servings: 4

Ingredient:

- 3 tbsp raw cane sugar
- 14 oz of mangoes
- 1 lime
- 3 sprigs of basil (or mint)
- 7 oz of raspberries
- 2 tbsp of honey
- ¼ cup mineral water (chilled)

Preparation:

1. In a small pot, bring the sugar and the 5 ounces of water to a boil. Continue to cook the mixture until it becomes syrupy, which should take about 10 minutes. Please allow it to cool.
2. While that is happening, peel the mangoes, cut the flesh into slices away from the pit, then roughly chop the flesh and place it in a tall container.
3. Squeeze the limes to extract the juice, then add two tablespoons of the juice and the syrup to the mangoes. Use an immersion blender to achieve a smooth consistency.
4. Rinse the basil, pat it dry with a towel, then pluck the leaves and coarsely chop them. Blend for a few seconds to combine after adding to mango puree. Put the mixture into an ice cream maker and let it freeze for about an hour.
5. While that is happening, sort through the raspberries in a separate container, combine them with the honey and the mineral water, and then puree the mixture using an immersion blender.
6. A bowl should be prepared with the raspberry puree after it has been strained through a fine-mesh sieve.
7. Make balls out of the mango sorbet using a scoop, and serve them immediately with raspberry sauce.

Nutritional values Calories: 164 kcal, Protein: 1g, Fat: 1g, Carbohydrates: 35g.

92. Chilled Buttermilk Soup

Preparation time: 20 minutes
Cooking time: 1 hour 20 minutes.
Servings: 4

Ingredient:

- 1 ½ pounds blueberries (fresh or frozen)
- 1 lemon
- 3 tbsp of cane sugar
- 2 tbsp crème de cassis (or cassis syrup)
- 1 ¾ liter buttermilk
- 2 tbsp of honey
- ¾ cup soy milk
- 1 oz amaretti cookies

Preparation:

1. Drain the blueberries thoroughly after rinsing, and allow the frozen berries to thaw. After being washed in hot water, the lemon should have its peel finely grated before being used. Put some pressure on the lemon. In a pot, bring two tablespoons' worth of lemon juice, two-thirds of the blueberries, the sugar, and either the cassis or the syrup to a boil. Cook, occasionally stirring, for five minutes over medium heat.
2. The mixture should be forced through a fine sieve into a bowl using a spoon to extract the maximum amount of juice possible.
3. After straining the liquid, add the remaining blueberries and allow the mixture to cool completely.
4. Buttermilk, honey, soy creamer, and lemon zest should all be mixed and stirred until smooth. Refrigerate for at least an hour. To serve, place a dollop of the blueberry compote in the center of each soup plate, then divide the chilled soup among the plates. Amaretti should be crumbled and sprinkled on top.

Nutritional values Calories: 336 kcal, Protein: 9g, Fat: 12g, Carbohydrates: 42g.

93. Strawberry Chocolate Clafoutis

Preparation time: 15 minutes
Cooking time: 40 minutes.
Servings: 6

Ingredient:

- 18 oz of strawberries
- 1 ½ oz butter
- 1 tsp of butter (for the mold)
- 3 ½ oz dark chocolate (at least 75% cocoa solids)
- ½ vanilla pod
- 3 eggs
- 7 oz whole wheat spelled flour
- 1 tbsp of cocoa powder
- 3 tbsp whole cane sugar
- 10 oz of milk (whole)
- 2 sprigs of mint
- 1 tsp of powdered sugar made from raw cane sugar

Preparation:

1. Strawberry preparation involves rinsing, cutting in half, and drying with paper towels. In a mold that has been greased, distribute half of the berries. To make the dough, break up the chocolate bar and melt it with 1.5 ounces of butter in a bowl set over a pot of simmering water. The vanilla bean should be halved along its length, and the pulp should be removed using a knife. Eggs should be separated. Egg whites that have been beaten to a stiff consistency.
2. Egg yolks, flour, cocoa powder, sugar, vanilla pulp, and milk should all be mixed and beaten until smooth. Mix until it forms a liquid dough with the chocolate butter, then fold the beaten egg whites.
3. After pouring the mixture over the berries, continue by layering the remaining strawberries on top of the mixture. Bake for twenty-five minutes in an oven that has been preheated to 350 °Fahrenheit.

4. After washing and drying the mint, remove the leaves. After removing the clafoutis from the oven, sprinkle it with powdered sugar and then garnish it with mint.

Nutritional values Calories: 340 kcal, Protein: 10g, Fat: 17g, Carbohydrates: 37g.

94. Heavenly Banana Slices

Preparation time: 10 minutes
Servings: 4

Ingredients:

- 6 bananas

For the dough:

- 6 eggs
- 4 ½ oz powdered sugar
- 4 ½ oz of flour
- ½ lemon (organic, zest)

For the cream:

- 1 ½ butter
- Vanilla pudding (made from 2 cup milk without sugar)

For the glaze:

- 3 ½ tbsp milk
- 4 ½ oz sugar
- 5 oz of chocolate
- 7 oz of butter

Preparation:

1. To make the dough, beat six egg yolks, sixty grams of sugar, and a little lemon zest until light and fluffy. First, gently combine the snow and the yolk dust, and then fold the sifted flour into the mixture. Whisk together six egg whites and sixty grams of sugar until stiff peaks form.
2. Spread the biscuit mixture across the bottom of a baking pan prepared with baking paper and measures 30 by 40 centimeters. Bake for about 12 to 15 minutes at 360 °F using hot air. Relax and take it easy.
3. Make the pudding according to the instructions on the package, then set it aside to cool before using it to make the cream. Repeated stirring will prevent skin from forming on the liquid.

4. Mix the almost-cold pudding with the butter and sugar after thoroughly beating them.
5. Peel approximately six bananas, cut them in half lengthwise, and slice them very thinly. Banana slices should be used to cover the dough in this recipe.
6. To make the icing, chop the chocolate bar into small pieces and then melt it with the butter in a bowl set over a pan of warm water. The next step is to combine sugar and milk into a smooth sauce while stirring until the sugar is completely dissolved.
7. After the cream has cooled, spread it on top. In the end, cover everything with the glaze.
8. The banana slices should be left to simmer. If possible, leave it overnight.

Nutritional value Calories: 215, Fat: 20g; Carbohydrates: 11g, Protein: 2g.

95. Blueberry Owl Pancakes

Preparation time: 5 minutes
Cooking time: 5 minutes.
Servings: 1

Ingredient:

- 1¼ cup nut milk
- 1/3 cup blueberries
- 1½ cups spelled, Kamut or amaranth flour
- 2 tbsp grapeseed oil
- 3 tbsp date sugar agave syrup

Preparation:

1. To prevent lumps from forming, date sugar and flour should be thoroughly combined. After adding the grapeseed oil and nut milk, mix the ingredients until a lumpy mixture is formed.
2. When adding the blueberries, ensure not to overmix the batter; instead, use a spatula to gently fold them so the lumps remain.
3. Grapeseed oil should be brushed into a large pan before it is heated.
4. After pouring the batter onto the pan, use the spatula to spread it into the desired shape and form.
5. After about three minutes of cooking, check to see if the bottom has turned golden and the edges have begun to brown.
6. Cook for approximately 2 minutes on the other side after turning the meat. Step 7
7. Serve with a variety of fruits and syrup made from agave.

Nutrition value Calories: 113 Fat: 5g, Carbohydrates: 14g, Protein: 3g.

96. Kamut Breakfast Porridge

Preparation time: 5 minutes
Cooking time: 12 minutes.
Servings: 4

Ingredient:

- 1 cup of Kamut or if you measure 7 oz
- 3 ¾ cups soft jelly coconut milk or nut milk (whichever is available or your preference),
- 4 tbsps agave syrup
- 1 tbsp of coconut oil.

Preparation:

1. In a blender, combine the kamut. It should not be smoothed, but rather cracked. After milling, the cracked Kamut should yield approximately 114 cups.
2. Now combine cracked Kamut, coconut or walnut milk (depending on personal preference or availability), in a mixing bowl. Then continue to stir until they are completely combined. You could do this in a bowl or a saucepan.
3. Heat the mixture for about 10 minutes. Allow it to boil over high heat for a few seconds before lowering it. Stir frequently until the desired thickness is reached.
4. After removing it from the heat, stir in either agave syrup or coconut oil to your boiled Kamut mixture. You could then top it with fresh fruits if desired. Your Kamut porridge is now ready to eat.

Nutrition value (per serving) Calories: 50 Fat: 0.2g, Carbohydrates: 11g, Protein: 1.4g.

97. Fruit Salad with Poppy Seed Yogurt

Preparation time: 10 minutes
Cooking time: 10 minutes.
Servings: 4

Ingredients:

For the fruit salad

- 1 baby pineapple - peel and cut into bite-sized pieces
- 1 small Galia melon - cut in half, cut out balls with a Parisian spoon (or cut into bite-sized pieces)
- 1 organic orange - peel and cut into bite-sized pieces
- 1 apple - wash and cut into bite-sized pieces
- 2 passion fruits - scrape out the pulp, including the seeds, with a spoon
- ½ pomegranate - scrape out the stones with a spoon
- 10 mint leaves - finely cut + 4 tips for decoration

For the poppy seed yogurt

- 4 oz soy yogurt (e.g. from Soyana)
- 2 tbsp poppy seeds
- 1 tsp organic orange zest
- ¼ tsp vanilla powder
- 1 pinch of cardamom powder

Preparation:

4. Mix all the ingredients - except the passion fruit - in a bowl for the fruit salad.
5. Mix all the ingredients in a small bowl for the poppy seed yogurt.
6. Divide the fruit salad into 4 bowls, top with the poppy seed yogurt, then the passion fruit, and enjoy garnished with the mint tips.

Nutrition value (per serving) Calories: 65 Carbohydrates: 10g, Protein: 6g.

98. Zucchini Bread Pancakes

Preparation time: 10 minutes
Cooking time: 10 minutes.
Servings: 10

Ingredient:

- 2 cups spelled or Kamut flour
- 2 tbsp sugar date
- 1/4 cup mashed banana burro
- 1 cup finely grated zucchini
- 1 cup nut milk
- 1/2 cup chopped walnuts
- 1 tbsp grape seed oil

Preparation:

1. In a large mixing bowl, combine the flour and date sugar.
2. Bring in the nut milk and mashed banana burro. Stir until everything is combined, scraping the bottom of the bowl to ensure there are no dry mix pockets. Stir in the courgette slices and walnuts.
3. In a griddle or skillet, heat the grapefruit oil over medium heat.
4. Place the pancakes on the hot grill. Cook for 4 to 5 minutes on each side.
5. Serve with agave syrup and enjoy!

Nutrition value Calories: 110 Fat: 5g, Carbohydrates: 13g, Protein: 4g.

99. Pancakes with Vanilla Sauce and Fruits

Preparation time: 40 minutes
Cooking time: 1 hour.
Servings: 4

Ingredients:

For the pancakes

- 9 oz wholemeal spelled flour
- 1 tsp Baking powder
- 3 tbsp sugar
- 2 cups soy drink
- 2 tbsp margarine, vegan + heat-resistant - let it become liquid

For the vanilla sauce

- 1 cup soy drink
- 6 tbsp soy cream
- 5 tsp organic corn starch, coated - mix with 4 tbsp water
- ½ tsp vanilla powder
- 1 pinch of organic lemon zest
- 2 tbsp agave syrup

Moreover

- 2 tbsp peanut oil, heat-resistant - fill into a small bowl
- 10 oz of seasonal fruits - wash and cut
- 2 tbsp sugar - grind finely in a blender

Preparation:

1. Put all the ingredients in a tall container for the pancakes and stir vigorously with a whisk or whisk. Then let the dough rest for 5 minutes.
2. In the meantime, put the soy drink in a saucepan for the sauce and bring it to a boil. Then add the remaining ingredients - except for the starch - and simmer for 2 minutes. Set aside and only boil again before consumption and stir in the starch.
3. Heat a pan and brush the bottom with peanut oil. Then add some of the batters with a spoon and fry small pancakes. Then place it on a large plate and cover it with a kitchen towel to keep it warm.
4. Arrange the pancakes with the vanilla sauce and the fruit, put the ground sugar in a sieve, sprinkle over the pancakes and serve.

Nutrition value Calories: 120 Fat: 6g, Carbohydrates: 15g, Protein: 6g.

100. Greek Yoghurt with Blueberries, Nuts, and Honey

Preparation time: 5 minutes
Servings: 4

Ingredient:

- 3 cups of greek unusual yogurt
- 1½ cups blueberries
- ¾ cup chopped mixed nuts
- ½ cup honey

Preparation:

- Place a dollop of yogurt in each of the bowls. Honey should be drizzled over the top after the blueberries and nuts have been sprinkled.

Nutritional value Calories: 457, Fat: 18g, Carbohydrates: 62g, Protein: 15g.

THE 30-DAY MEAL PLAN

DAY	BREAKFAST	LUNCH	DINNER
DAY 1	Mushroom Frittata	Lentil-Lamb Ragu	Shrimp With Spicy Spinach
DAY 2	Eggs And Fruit Salad	Lamb Chops With Mustard And Garlic	Vegetable Soup
DAY 3	Coconut Pancakes	Baked Sweet Potato Soup	Salmon And Roasted Asparagus
DAY 4	Oatmeal Spiced With Apple Pie	Salmon With Brown Rice And Spinach	Persimmon And Pear Salad
DAY 5	Orange Apple Breakfast Shake	Almond Chicken	Eggs And Fruit Salad
DAY 6	Buckwheat Waffles	Wholemeal Pasta With Tomato Sauce And Basil	Quick Chicken Stir-Fry
DAY 7	Spicy Quinoa	Chicken With Mustard And Honey	Broccoli And Lentil Stew
DAY 8	Sweet Potato Hash	Chicken Skewers With Mint Sauce	Pecan-Crusted Trout
DAY 9	Grapefruit Breakfast	Coconut Chicken	Avocado And Mango Salad
DAY 10	Spinach Muffins	Mushroom Risotto	Sautéed Shrimp
DAY 11	Eggs And Apple Pork With Strawberries	Barbecue Chicken Salad	Swordfish With Pineapple And Coriander
DAY 12	Chocolate Cherry Smoothie	Roasted Chicken Wraps	Low Carb Zucchini Lasagne Vegetarian

DAY 13	Gingerbread Oatmeal	Spicy Chicken Drumsticks	Quick And Easy Pumpkin Soup
DAY 14	Buckwheat Crepes With Berries	Swordfish With Pineapple And Coriander	Whitefish With Spice Removal
DAY 15	Oatmeal Spiced With Apple Pie	Chicken Curry	Lemon-Scented Steamed Salmon With Zucchini
DAY 16	Spicy Quinoa	Citrus Salmon On A Bed Of Vegetables	Buddha Bowl
DAY 17	Eggs And Fruit Salad	Roasted Chicken With Lemon And Sage	Pad Thai Noodles With Buckwheat
DAY 18	Grapefruit Breakfast	Chicken And Vegetable Skewers	Pad Thai Noodles With Buckwheat
DAY 19	Buckwheat Waffles	Salmon And Roasted Asparagus	Chopped Mediterranean Salad
DAY 20	Coconut Pancakes	Chicken Skewers With Mint Sauce	Cauliflower Soup With Roasted Garlic
DAY 21	Sweet Potato Hash	Swordfish With Pineapple And Coriander	Stir-Fried Tofu And Spinach
DAY 22	Eggs And Apple Pork With Strawberries	Cevics Salmon	Turmeric Chicken Salad
DAY 23	Mushroom Frittata	Chicken With Mustard And Honey	Alkaline Spring Salad
DAY 24	Chocolate Cherry Smoothie	Almond Chicken	Shrimp With Cinnamon Sauce
DAY 25	Spinach Muffins	Baked Salmon Steak Steaks	Arlecchino Salad

DAY 26	Gingerbread Oatmeal	Lamb Chops With Mustard And Garlic	Roasted Broccoli And Cashews
DAY 27	Buckwheat Waffles	Chicken And Vegetable Skewers	Vegetable Soup
DAY 28	Buckwheat Crepes With Berries	Barbecue Chicken Salad	Fried Rice With Cabbage
DAY 29	Grapefruit Breakfast	Salmon With Quinoa	Deli Soup And A Roll
DAY 30	Coconut Pancakes	Roasted Chicken Wraps	Shrimp With Cinnamon Sauce

GET YOUR BONUS NOW!

SCAN THE QR CODE BELOW

Printed in Great Britain
by Amazon

19119899R00075